"Finally a book on getting new prospects into your pipeline that tells you not only what to do but HOW to do it. Kendra Lee's *The Sales Magnet* is a must read for everyone tired of endless cold calls, poor results, and sleepless nights."

—John Doerr, President RAIN Group and *Wall Street Journal* Best-Selling Author of *Rainmaking Conversations*

"Instead of teaching you how to find prospects who are ready to buy using techniques equivalent to helping you find a needle in a haystack, Kendra Lee's new book *The Sales Magnet* shows you how to run a gigantic magnet through the haystack so that the needle comes to you."

—Jeff Arnold, MAM, CAE; Executive Director of The Sales Association

"Kendra Lee has done it again! To use Kendra's own words, *The Sales Magnet* is a grabber. It catches your attention from the beginning and then leads you to action. If you want more success, then learn from the best. Kendra lives what she preaches and does it like no other can. You will have success by applying the principles in this book."

—Douglas Edwards, President, TestOut Corporation

"Kendra Lee is a sales champion. In the pages of this book she cuts through the confusion and lays out a plan, with real action oriented strategies you can put to work for yourself, in your business, and your sales career. If you want to sell more, with far less resistance then don't just own this book, but literally devour it."

—Josh Hinds, Speaker & author of *It's Your Life, LIVE BIG!* www.JoshHinds.com

"*The Sales Magnet* by Kendra Lee should be required reading. There are a handful of heavy hitters offering sales and marketing consulting to professional services companies. What sets Kendra apart—and way ahead of the rest—is that she offers a client-centered, consultative, solution oriented approach that seeks to find the best methods for her *client*, the seller."

—Chris Boyle, MyITpros

"If you are tired of staring at empty sales pipelines and/or working with the wrong type of prospects, pick this book up today. This 'how-to' book will get your sales jump started in the right direction. Stop being the best kept secret and learn how to become a magnet!"

—Colleen Stanley, Chief Selling Officer, SalesLeadership, Inc.

"Kendra Lee's *The Sales Magnet* is a blue print for lead generation in today's still difficult selling environment. Kendra is the go-to thought leader for cutting edge strategies on email and social media channels. Run (don't walk) to get your copy of this powerful new, information-packed book. And while you're there, pick up a copy for every member of your team."

—Wendy Weiss, The Queen of Cold Calling™

"Kendra's book is a must for every sales professional. It gives excellent ideas on finding new opportunities and a series of effective and focused actions that make those very important potential clients want to listen to your offering. We have been able to attract a greater number of the right type of prospects, which I'm sure will make a real impact on our sales results."

—Muntsa Cuchí-Robinson, Sales Director
at CPSL – Language Solutions.

"As a sales leadership consultant, I see struggling salespeople every week using the same old efforts to build their pipelines and achieve quota. After previewing Kendra Lee's new book *The Sales Magnet* this should no longer be the case! In this book you will find practical step-by-step approaches to move beyond simple prospecting into creating personal market dominance."

—Ken Thoreson, Acumen Management Group,
Your Sales Management Guru

"Kendra Lee ends the 'cold call reluctance' cycle of avoidance, guilt, and then desperation! She has identified tools that sellers recognize are available but haven't tapped into for lack of knowledge and perceived ease. The good news the strategies she identifies in this book are well explained and totally demystified. A must-read for anyone who is ready to put some of their 'calling hours' to better use."

—Andrea Waltz, Co-Author, *Go for No! Yes is the*
Destination, No is How You Get There

"Kendra gets it! Her book is spot-on in providing the guidance and direction we all need to be able to attract customers in today's market. What makes the ideas work so well is Kendra's background. She got into sales not as a 'born salesperson,' but rather as a reluctant salesperson who faced the same challenges that many other salespeople face. The difference is Kendra overcame these challenges to become incredibly successful. In this book, she shares her secrets!"

—Mark Hunter, The Sales Hunter
Author of *High-Profit Selling: Win the Sale*
Without Compromising on Price

"No matter what your level of expertise, or what industry you sell in, Kendra takes all the drama out of the sales process, and helps you put the puzzle pieces together. This book will give you clarity while building your skills and confidence."

—Marlene Chism, author of *Stop Workplace Drama*

"It seems to me that sales books are like London buses—there's one coming along every minute, but you always have to wait quite long time for one that will take you precisely where you need to go: *The Sales Magnet* will do that, so climb on board as soon as you can."

—Jonathan Farrington, Chairman, JF Corporation

"*The Sales Magnet* is a must read for those struggling to build their pipelines, and frustrated with dated 'smile and dial' strategies. Kendra describes a great process to refine your targets and engage them in a manner that will 'grab' them, without downright annoying them. If I could get all sales managers to think this way—pipelines would be a lot richer (literally and figuratively)!"

—Devon McDonald, Senior Associate at OpenView Venture Partners

"I just love how Kendra shares all these great ideas and tips to make prospecting so much more rewarding. Her approach to lead generation in this book is so practical and so perfect for selling in today's social media world. What a real pro!"

—Robin Carey, CEO, Social Media LLC

"What if prospects were drawn to you with an irresistible force? Kendra shares the secrets that let you ditch cold calling once and for all—so you can spend your valuable selling time talking with hot prospects instead. *The Sales Magnet* is for anyone who has said 'There has to be a better way!' There is, and you'll learn what it is, along with step-by-step details on how to do it."

—Nancy Nardin, President Smart Selling Tools

"If you still think you need to COLD CALL to be successful—well—Kendra is about to CHANGE YOUR MIND. She'll give you the kick-in-the-pants you need to attract piles of customers and you won't have to break a fingernail doing it! Now. Get reading her book!"

—Kim Duke www.salesdivas.com

"This book turns prospecting inside out. Attraction trifecta, grabbers, trigger events, prospecting interruptus may not be in your sales lexicon—but they should be! Chalked full of practical and proven detailed methodology with accompanying tips and tricks to succeed; you'll discover the best part is you order off the menu of what you believe will work best for you. *The Sales Magnet* will change how you do business. And you will do more business!"

—Clayton Shold, President, Salesopedia

"Pulling prospective buyers to you is a brilliant marketing and sales strategy. In *The Sales Magnet*, Kendra Lee provides strategy and practical how-tos for you to become magnetic! She uses her experience and best practices for tips that anyone can implement. It's more than a must-read book, it's a must-do!"

—Nancy Bleeke, Sales Pro Insider, Inc.

THE SALES MAGNET

How to Get More Customers Without Cold Calling

KENDRA LEE

With foreword by Jill Konrath

President, KLA Press: Kendra Lee

Book design by DesignForBooks.com

© 2013 by Kendra Lee

Published by KLA Press

Printed in the United States of America

Library of Congress Control Number: 2009903530

Publisher's Cataloging-in-Publication data

Lee, Kendra.
    The Sales magnet : how to get more customers without cold calling / Kendra Lee ; with foreword by Jill Konrath.
    p. cm.
    ISBN 978-0-9857829-1-7 (pbk.)
    Includes index.
    ISBN 978-0-9857829-2-4 (e-book: ePub)
    ISBN 978-0-9857829-3-1 (e-book: Kindle/Mobi)

1. Selling. 2. Success in business. 3. Selling--Psychological aspects. 4. Selling --Technique. I. Konrath, Jill. II. Title.

HF5438.25 .L42 2013
658.8/1 --dc23   2009903530

Visit us at: www.thesalesmagnet.com

Thank you . . .

*To our raving fans who share their trials and
tribulations of getting prospects to respond, ask for
advice, and not only share what failed, but
also what worked—then come back for more!*

*To all our clients who eagerly test my ideas and openly
offer their results and suggestions.*

*To my family, Bill, Bill, Michael and Jeff for their
wonderful support and belief in me.*

*You are each an inspiration to me and bring excitement to
every day. Lead generation is my passion. Thank you for
allowing me to share it with you!*

Contents

· ·

Foreword

W ithout prospects, there are no sales. Yet the changing market dynamics and struggling economy have turned the always challenging task of prospecting into a seemingly insurmountable hurdle.

For people who need lots of hot prospects to be successful, keeping the pipeline full can be daunting. Plus, for many entrepreneurs, it's simply not what they love to do.

So how can you ever get ahead of the game? Is it even possible? Or are you consigned to a lifetime of endless cold calling filled with minimal returns?

I know exactly how you feel—and it's not fun. Not too long ago, my own business crashed and I had to restart it from Ground Zero. But it was virtually impossible to reach potential buyers. Everyone was way too busy to want to meet with another self-serving salesperson.

Clearly new strategies were needed. Since my personal expertise was in selling to the corporate markets, I set out to discover what it took to crack into accounts when no one answered the phone and no one called you back. When I finally figured out what worked, I wrote *Selling to Big Companies*, a step-by-step primer to land bigger clients.

At the very same time, Kendra Lee was tackling the exact same challenge for people who sold to the SMB (small- and medium-sized business) market. *Selling Against the Goal,* her initial book, came out a month before mine from the very same publisher.

When I read it, I immediately knew she was a force to be reckoned with! I was impressed with her keen knowledge and track record of success. She'd thrown away the book on prospecting and started over with a fresh plan to get sales that didn't depend solely on cold calling.

Heresy, yes! But brilliant. Now, five years later, she's back with another game-changing book that's even better than her first one—*The Sales Magnet.* It's a practical, no-nonsense book filled with tons of examples she's helped her numerous clients implement.

You will benefit from the strategies in the book if you:

- Are tired of constantly struggling to find new opportunities. It's no fun to be scrambling to uncover viable companies who can use your products or services.

- Want to create a predictable revenue stream. By embracing these concepts, you'll be adding new prospects to your pipeline on a regular basis.

Start out by getting clear on your best target markets—those organizations that would realize value from your offering. You'll also want to focus in on trigger events that create urgency for what you sell and on crafting strong value propositions that really resonate with your prospects.

Then dive into the variety of prospect attraction strategies that are detailed in the book: Email prospecting, social networking, online events, events, and much more. Instead of making you feel guilty about not doing it all, you're encouraged to find the approach(es) that feel best for you—and then get started.

Finally, check out the incredible resource library that Kendra has created to support this book. She's included examples, sample plans, audio seminars, cheat sheets, guidelines, and more. This will cut hours off your planning time, enabling you to put all these ideas into practice right away.

By applying the strategies in *The Sales Magnet,* you'll find more opportunities than you ever thought possible—in a much shorter timeframe than you could ever imagine.

To your sales success,

Jill Konrath

Bestselling author of *Selling to Big Companies* and *SNAP Selling*

Introduction

In spite of starting my career in accounting, failing IBM's entry sales rep exam, getting a sales area that had failed to earn more than $300,000 in the previous three years combined, and being told I couldn't sell without an engineering background, I chose to become a seller and vowed to prove those naysayers wrong.

Yes, I started my sales career as an accountant. I know it sounds funny, but sellers come from varied backgrounds.

Many of you may be entrepreneurs who started your own businesses and were forced into sales to be successful. Or you were dragged into selling reluctantly because your job role changed. Some of you, like me, actually chose to make the move because sales sounded more exciting and lucrative.

Regardless of how we all got here, we're in sales with personal goals that require us to find prospects to achieve them. But where do we find those people? Most sales training programs begin with, "when you have a lead" or "as you begin your sales process." Short of telling you to make cold calls, they don't provide any advice on how to go about getting the leads you need.

That's exactly what happened to me. I was doing a great job as an IBM accountant with a promising career and a bright future. But, I felt like something was missing and I decided that being in sales might fill the gap.

In my first attempt to become a seller, I failed the technical engineering test and was told I couldn't possibly be successful in sales. I didn't have the technical aptitude and was sent away.

Then the opportunity presented itself. IBM underwent restructuring, offering everybody in the company the opportunity to try their hand at sales, with a "minor" string attached. If you weren't successful in sales, you wouldn't be allowed back into your old job. You were out!

Being young and willing to take a risk, I signed up to become a seller and began a yearlong sales training program. Within the first quarter, my manager determined it was time for me to step up and start selling. So, with three months of a 12-month program under my belt, I was thrown out into the wide world of sales—knowing that if I wasn't successful, I was out of the company.

That first year my quota was $1 million in a sales area that had earned a total of only $300,000 over the three previous years. I was expected to bring in brand new accounts—companies that were using no IBM products.

My sales area was no prize by IBM standards. It was a mishmash of small companies consisting of bowling alleys, local movie theaters, insurance agencies, CPA firms, law firms, consulting firms, and day care centers. I had nine different industries, all of which were highly unlikely buyers of any significant amount of computer equipment that would help me achieve my quota.

With an average sale of $15,000, I barely made goal in the last days of December.

It was painful, scary, and harder than I'd ever expected. I knew I had to find a smarter way—and I had two immediate problems to solve if I was going to be successful.

1. My prospects didn't know we had any solutions that fit their businesses. They saw IBM as an expensive, big-company solution. They didn't know we had offerings designed especially for small companies in their industries.

2. I had to find the people with a need. My sales area was huge and cold calling wasn't effective. It was a needle-in-the-haystack game.

The answer was simple. I had to be in front of my prospects when the problem hit, with an easy, non-threatening way for them to reach out to me.

The execution was harder.

With no marketing background, how could I catch executives' attention? Who should I target? What did they want to know about? How could I get them to respond to my non-cold calling approach? And when they had a need, how could I be sure they'd remember me and call?

And so the attraction strategies in this book evolved.

Starting with niche industries in my large sales area, I began to build awareness for myself and my offerings in each one. They learned who I was and started calling me about the business issues I profiled. They wanted someone knowledgeable who could help them address their challenges and they developed confidence in me.

The attraction strategies worked so well, I met my quota in September my second year and was named to IBM's Golden Circle, the elite award in sales. With so many leads coming in, I couldn't follow up on all of them and had to put new strategies in place to ensure I didn't miss any. By my third year, my attraction strategies grew that little mishmash sales area of unlikely buyers—who spent no more than $15,000–30,000 every three or four years—to over $9 million in annual revenue!

I wrote this book as a resource for you in attracting prospects from your list of small and midsize companies. I've included loads of tips, techniques, and examples you can use to successfully draw prospects to you. As you read, pick out those strategies that feel most comfortable to you and try them. You'll know right away what works for you and what doesn't.

I guarantee you that these strategies work. All you have to do is test them with your prospects and you'll see.

When I first began using attraction strategies in place of cold calling, the Web didn't exist. My options were limited to letters, faxes, events, networking, and referrals. Since that time the Internet has exploded and made it easier for sellers to reach their prospects. You just need to know how, and this book will tell you exactly what to do.

Your Sales Magnet

Because it's always easier to start from something, I've put together a wealth of electronic resources and tools that you can use in creating your attraction strategies. They're neatly assembled just for you in the Sales Magnet Tool Kit at www.thesalesmagnet.com.

You'll find fresh new tools and resources that I'm continually updating for you to use. I want to see you be as successful at attracting prospects as I have!

I struggled for two years figuring out how to attract new, qualified contacts without the laborious effort of cold calling. After all this time, I've never gone back to phone prospecting and you don't have to, either.

Use my ideas. Adapt them to the companies in your target segment. Learn from my mistakes and successes.

I know you'll find as much good fortune as I did. Soon you'll have the problem of too many leads coming your way. And that's a problem we're all happy to have!

Share Your Successes

I'm very interested to hear about your successes as you try ideas from this book. I look forward to hearing how you adapted them for your own markets and the results you achieved!

Share them with me at www.thesalesmagnet.com/share mysuccess and I'll feature YOUR story on our website.

Part 1

Prepare Yourself
for a Barrage of Prospects

So you've decided you need more leads.

Your funnel isn't nearly as full as you'd like. You're tired of cold calling.

It's time for a new strategy. It's time to get more hot prospects to come to you because they've heard of you or your company. They want to work with you. You're who they think can help them.

That's what I call prospect attraction. New contacts respond to your lead generation activities. They email you, attend your webinars, read your blogs, and watch your social network comments.

They learn your name and what your company does. You elevate yourself to be the expert they listen to even before you know who they are.

Suddenly, you have a barrage of prospects at your virtual door, each clamoring to discuss how you could help them.

Sound like what you're looking for? Well let's make it happen.

It all begins with changing the way you view prospecting and lead generation. And it starts here.

1

Why Prospecting
Is No Picnic

. . . .

G rab a cup of coffee and let's talk.
Prospecting is no picnic. While you like speaking with
new contacts, getting their attention is the challenge. They're
busy people and they just don't have time for you. You have
outstanding offerings and know you can make a difference in
their business with the references to prove it!

But you can't get new contacts to notice you, and mean-
while your pipeline is suffering.

Doesn't it sometimes feel as if there are never enough
customers to fill your funnel? Then you fret, wondering how
you're going to reach your goals?

Have you cold-called yourself to death and think that
there's got to be a better way?

I work with a lot of people who are struggling with this.
Take Bob for example. He's in sales and constantly scrambling
to fill his pipeline. He hates cold calling and prefers to spend
his time with customers. He closes good-sized deals but never
has enough new opportunities to meet his sales goals.

Sandy just started her company two years ago. She has
very satisfied customers and a great consulting team and she

longs to take her business to higher levels through expansion into more regions. She needs a strategy to penetrate new markets and is uncertain what to do.

Matt's sales area is comprised of too many companies to count. While he's responsible for new business development, he can't begin to call every one. He's wrangling with how to attract those organizations that have an immediate need.

Then there's Amy, who has an established firm with talented employees all involved in supporting customers and with little extra time for selling. She's striving to feed them enough fresh, qualified prospects to meet the company's revenue objectives.

Does one of these people sound like you? You know what they're facing, don't you? And it's painful. It's a never-ending prospecting cycle where you feel you can't get ahead of the game.

You're constantly worrying about when you'll have time to prospect and if there will enough new opportunities in your pipeline. You're faced with the challenge of how to balance customer responsibilities with business development requirements.

What options do you have?

So what can you do? What choices are available to you?

You know you could cold call, yet who wants to do that? Frankly, nobody.

People don't call you back. You aren't sure you're calling the right person. Gatekeepers block you from connecting with decision-makers. It's stressful, time-consuming, and definitely no picnic.

You could hire a telemarketer. Maybe you've even done it before. You know others who have. The challenge with having other people call on your behalf is that they don't know your business like you do. They miss obvious opportunities, bungle your value proposition, and set appointments with unqualified contacts. You spend tons of time educating a telemarketer only to have the whole thing fail.

What a waste of effort and money.

Of course there are always referrals, but you need a bunch of them to drive the sales volume you have in mind. You ask, and ask, and ask. Some clients provide good ones. Many don't know who to refer you to. If you do get the name of a new contact, it's often someone who may buy someday but has no need today.

While you like knowing you have future potential in your pipeline, it doesn't help meet today's objectives.

You know you need a strategy to fill your pipeline, but you need something simpler that will be more successful in drawing clients.

Stop the Treadmill

What you really want is to attract prospects and eliminate the wasted effort. The good news is that you can while reaping greater rewards.

There are a whole slew of ways to connect with those people you want to be your customers and proven strategies that'll catch their attention and have them clamoring to talk with you. They'll recognize how you can help and actually request that you call them.

Instead of cold calling you can use email, webcasts, blogs, social networking, public relations, and more. Create follow-up strategies that'll nurture prospects until they're ready to talk with you. I'll teach you all of them.

I'm going to give you a bunch of ideas for enticing new prospects. Forget any stipulation that the only way to be successful in prospecting is through cold calling. It's your choice how you want to get your value proposition in front of companies and capture their interest. I'll show you lots of ways and give you straightforward how-to tips in every chapter.

You decide how much time you want to spend prospecting. Determine what aligns best with your objectives. One client I work with can only manage four leads a month; others require hundreds.

In my experience most sellers really require only 10–20 new opportunities every 30 days to achieve their goals. You want to figure out how many leads you need, then create an attraction strategy to bring them to you. I'll show you how to secure them in the way that's simplest for you.

If you aren't sure how many leads you need, use the Quota Gap Calculator in the Sales Magnet Tool Kit on my website to figure it out in less than 10 minutes.

Before you know it you'll be using these attraction strategies and drawing prospects to you, telling you they want to talk about how you can assist them. And then your issue won't be filling your pipeline. It'll be following up on all those leads!

Now that's a nice challenge to have.

Ignore the Skeptics!

I get asked all the time, can you really get new leads without cold calling? Sellers and experts alike are skeptical.

One afternoon I went into great detail with a sales consultant explaining how you absolutely can use email and other non-phone techniques to get contacts to reach out and ask you to sell to them. I thought she had finally seen the light about how prospect attraction can work, until I read the blog where she posted her interview with me.

She wrote: "Does email prospecting work? Kendra says yes, if done with the right *other* proactive activities like calling."

I just shook my head in disappointment. She'd missed the point.

Don't get me wrong. When there's a top prospect you absolutely must secure an appointment with, you definitely need to call.

But when you have a group of contacts who are similar and you're trying to identify interested prospects, attraction strategies are the way to go. You can reach out to them using a very tailored message and approach that engages those who want to know more to reply to you.

The consultant didn't want to believe that you really can allure buyers who choose you and request your help.

I'm here to tell you that you can get prospects to jump up and say, "Take me! Call me! I need your help!" I'm going to show you how to use attraction strategies to do just that so you fill your pipeline with people who already know they want to work with you.

No more cold calling with a hope and a prayer—and a shudder of reluctance.

Sales Magnet Tools for You

If you aren't sure how many leads you need, check out the Quota Gap Calculator in the Sales Magnet Tool Kit. You'll know the answer in just 10 minutes or less!

Throughout the book you'll see this section wherever I've assembled electronic resources that'll help you in creating your attraction strategies. They're all included in the Sales Magnet Tool Kit at www.thesalesmagnet.com.

2

Attract
Prospects to You

The real problem in prospecting is that your contacts don't know you.

Even if they have a need, they don't know you're out there and that they really should be talking with you. They're sitting back ignoring what should be fixed or turning to Internet searches and their network for solutions.

You have to be in front of your prospects when they recognize they have a problem. If you're right there, they'll ask for your guidance and recommendations. You'll become the trusted advisor who helps them map out the answer, determine their budget, and make it all work. If you show up late, they're already working with someone else. You find yourself in a competitive situation, selling against someone who's already achieved honored status.

There definitely are times when you should help create desire. But when you have an empty pipeline, you can't wait around nurturing and coaxing your prospect until he sees the light and wants to address the issue. You need new opportunities now.

Your focus must be on finding those people who realize they have a problem and are just beginning their search for an answer. These are the ideal contacts you want to attract. And to catch their attention, they have to know about you.

That's why prospecting is so hard.

We know we're trying to find someone who has a qualified need, but it's often as if you're shooting darts at a dartboard—blindfolded—after being turned around in a circle five times. Of all those potential customers out there, which ones have recognized they have an issue? And how do you make sure they've heard of you?

In my first sales area I covered nine different industries and had thousands of small and midsize companies that I was responsible for breaking into that year. From law firms to bowling alleys, it was overwhelming to think about how I could possibly find those businesses that had determined they were ready to invest in a new computer system. Because there were so many, there was no way they'd know to call me when they were investigating a purchase unless I did something about it.

I had my own personal dartboard but no darts.

All this means is that you have two objectives in prospecting:

1. Make yourself known in the markets where your best prospects can be found

2. Attract prospects who have a problem you can solve

All along you've known you must find the contacts who have issues, but you've probably never thought about making yourself known to them. This book will help you with both. To get your name out in so many places may seem like a daunting proposition to you as it did to me, but it's achievable.

If you start in small bites, you can do it and I'll show you how.

Enter the Attraction Trifecta

To get you started let's look at three sets of attraction strategies, the Attraction Trifecta as I call it.

In horseracing a trifecta is a race where you place bets on three horses to finish first, second, and third. If you think about it, you're in a race to find enough new opportunities to meet your sales goals. You're betting on yourself to fill a pipeline with prospects who are interested in working with you because they think you can help them.

The Attraction Trifecta gives you three sets of powerful strategies to get your name out in front of your target companies and entice new contacts to you. Combined over time, as you continue to use them you'll become a well-known expert in your field. Even if you change territories, companies or products, so many people will know of you that they'll think of you when they're looking to solve a problem. They'll call you to ask if you can help or if you can recommend someone who can.

New prospects will seek you out. When that happens, you've made it. You've won the Attraction Trifecta.

What are the three magnetic strategies in the Attraction Trifecta that will draw prospects to you?

1. **Personal**—Personal attraction strategies make the prospect feel like you've reached out to make

a personal connection, such as email, letters, networking and phone pursuit.

2. **Digital**—Digital strategies use internet tools and resources to reach your prospects, such as e-newsletters, articles, social networking, blogging, and on-line public relations.

3. **Collaborative**—Collaborative strategies engage together with others to capture prospects' interest through online and local events, off-line public relations, and alliance partnerships.

Certainly cold calling and referrals are options, and there are some very good resources on both. But this book is designed for those of you who are tired of cold calling, already know how to secure referrals, and want to start drawing leads to you using novel approaches.

The secret behind the Attraction Trifecta strategies is in their power to work together to reach your market. You can combine them to stay in front of your prospects without seeming repetitive. Each place they go, your name pops up: On a social networking site linked to someone they know, as a quote in a blog post they're reading, or in an email you sent them.

Every person is unique, and so too are your prospects. Some people respond better to email, others a handwritten note or an invitation, others to articles they found during research. By mixing up your approaches using the Trifecta, you're more likely to connect. And even better, you appear ubiquitous—everywhere they turn, there you are!

They begin asking themselves, "Do we have that problem after all? Should we be talking to you?" Bulls-eye! You have a lead.

You Have My Permission

Are all these ideas beginning to sound intimidating to you? If so, take a deep breath, a sip of coffee, and let's step back.

You don't need to try all the concepts in this book. What's most important is that you get started. Begin to get your name out in front of your potential customers so they'll know to call you when they require assistance.

Not every attraction strategy in the Trifecta will feel comfortable for you.

Take public speaking as an example. Some people never can imagine themselves standing in front of a local chamber of commerce or association and giving a presentation, even though they are quite knowledgeable. Some people enjoy sharing their expertise from a stage and having people crowd around to talk with them afterward. They seek out conference and trade show speaking opportunities. This may not be your thing, and that's okay.

Instead, you may enjoy writing and you gravitate toward blogging and articles. Or you may like being spontaneous and prefer to whip up a series of emails, update your profile on a social network, or send a quick handwritten note. If your best prospects tend to be technical, Web events may be the best avenue to give them the depth of information they need before seeking you out.

Whatever your preference, it's your choice.

If you aren't confident in an attraction strategy, it probably won't be successful for you. So skip over it. Choose the strategies that take advantage of your innate abilities.

You don't have to try them all at once. You don't even have to do more than one thing. You can be more powerful using all three, however even if you choose only one strategy within the Trifecta you can still win the race.

As you begin each chapter in this book, figure out which techniques sound like the most fun and play to your strengths. Skip a particular strategy if it feels too foreign for you to consider.

Read about those ideas you know you'd like to use. Consider how you'd execute them in your selling. Think about your prospects and the resources available to you and begin to picture yourself implementing the strategies. How would you do it?

Ask yourself:

- What do I need to do to execute it?
- How long would it take me?
- What resources would I need?
- How would my customers respond?
- How many new prospects do I think I could get?

Visualize the strategy working for you. Bring it to life in your mind and have fun with it! Put your personal flare into it.

Don't stop with the attraction strategies you know you want to use. Challenge yourself to try some that sound interesting but might stretch you a bit.

Choose one and jump in. Worst case, it doesn't yield any new prospects. Best case, you discover a hidden gold mine and put your name out in front of your market in a new way!

You have my permission to try the techniques you think will best fit you. The key is to begin, and you only need to start with *one*.

3

Get Your Focus

. . . .

If you're reading this book, you've already decided cold calling isn't your best approach to attracting prospects.

You probably have a large contact base you're supposed to mine for opportunities. It's so big you can't begin to call everyone. It'd take you more than a year to call through the whole list even once!

You'd love a way to simplify your lead generation efforts and get prospects to come to you with less frustration and more success. The Attraction Trifecta is your answer. It will give you the strategies to allure new buyers, but first you must find your focus.

What do I mean by focus? Why can't you just jump in and start sending emails? Because every prospect is different.

If you try to say the same thing to each prospect on your list, you'll end up with a generic message that's no better than a TV commercial. One seller I know calls it "spray and pray." Your response rates will be no better than when you're dialing for dollars from a phonebook. No matter how artfully composed your email, event, or social network comment, if the message isn't targeted to your prospects' needs, they'll see right through it.

You have to find your focus first. And to do that, you need to know:

- Which prospects might have an immediate need?
- How are they similar?
- What are their issues?
- Why would they want to talk with you?
- What makes them good prospects for you?

These are the questions you must ask yourself every time you start your prospect attraction efforts.

When I was selling to nine different industries, it was impossible to fathom how to identify who had a need. There were more than 10,000 companies in my area. Clearly I wasn't going to contact every one. Of course, it didn't stop me from trying.

I called to introduce myself and my company, looking for a challenge I could address, a pain they were experiencing and an opportunity to talk about what I sold. Guess how many leads I found? Yep, you got it. None.

It was the proverbial needle-in-the-haystack. After a year of that approach and barely achieving my quota on the last few days of the year, I craved a different approach. I had to find my focus, just like you.

Visualize the Trees—Not Just the Forest

It's time to stop viewing your prospects as a forest and to begin to enjoy the subtleties of the trees. You may have maples, pines, and aspens. Have you noticed how each kind is unique? Their leaves, heights, and climates all vary. You wouldn't build a tree house the same way in each variety of trees. Nor will you approach your prospects in a similar manner.

You require a strategy that'll allow you to divide your contact base into manageable groups of people who have similar characteristics and needs that you can address and who are most likely to require your services. You want to target those segments where you have the best opportunity to get business in the door, identifying a micro-set of companies that'll require the least amount of time and money to secure the highest return for your efforts.

I call these groups your target markets.

Your goal in focusing attraction strategies on a few defined target markets is to:

- Create an awareness for you and your company within test groups

- Establish your credibility

- Attract businesses that have a need to respond to you

To define your target markets, take a closer look at your list of contacts and begin by arranging them in groups with similar characteristics.

Common characteristic groupings to consider include:

- Industry (medical, legal, manufacturing)

- Size (revenue, number of employees, locations, users, desktops, phone lines)

- Geographic location (city, state, region, country)

- Titles you most frequently sell to (CIO, IT manager, office manager, CFO, business owner)

- Departments that typically buy from you
  (Operations, Information Technology, Legal,
  Human Resources, Purchasing)

Think about what you sell to different companies.

- Which ones are buying similar solutions?
- What's common about those customers?
- Are they all from the same industry, work in the
  same types of departments, have similar numbers
  of employees?

When I was selling computer solutions, my recommendations tended to align by industry and company size. Small
bowling alleys usually needed the same software and services.
But law offices required another type of software, more complex hardware, and managed support services. I divided my
eclectic sales area by industry and number of employees to
create separate bowling alley and legal target markets.

For each one I was able to devise an approach and message
that fit its unique characteristics and needs.

In spite of the extra work, it felt so much more comfortable because I was no longer trying to fit a common strategy to
very unique companies. The added bonus was that those target
markets started to notice me. Prospect attraction had begun!

Common Target Market Choices
that Could Work For You

If you aren't sure what your target markets should be, not to
worry. Most sellers find their own prospects fall into three

common categories. Choose one of these.

1. **Industry**—This is what I used because the solutions and needs were significantly different based on the industry my client was in. Typically you include a company size parameter as well. Without another parameter, your group tends to be too broad for you to effectively focus your attraction strategy. Even if the same strategy *will* fit all companies in that industry, the sheer size of the group tends to be too large to focus on. In either situation, you need another way to slice the target market and decrease the size, creating a micro-segment.

2. **Company size**—Here you select a group based on companies all of a similar size, for example revenue, number of employees, or users. Some sellers use the size of a specific department, such as Finance, Human Resources or Information Technology. Many organizations use company size as their primary target market definition. This is effective when your solutions are used similarly across many industries and your prospects have similar needs.

3. **Partner target markets**—If you are aligned closely with another company, like Microsoft, Hewlett-Packard or a franchise, they often have defined segments that you can use, too. This allows you to leverage their materials, and possibly their lists, for your attraction efforts.

I've always preferred a combination of industry and company size as my first cut for a target market. Companies who are the same size within one industry often have similar needs and use our solutions in like ways.

We sell sales consulting and training services to small and mid-market businesses focused on new client acquisition. We also have a specialization in the information technology (IT) industry. The sales issues that small and medium-sized IT companies are grappling with as they grow their businesses tend to be alike. But what Hewlett-Packard and Apple need is quite different than their channel partners. Rather than attempt to treat them the same because they both fall within the IT industry, I segment our list by size to refine our message and approach to better fit the sales issues in prospects' businesses.

These commonalities of smaller micro-segments make it easy to focus our attraction strategy messages in manners that appear very personal to prospects. And the more personal it feels, the more likely they are to begin to notice me!

These aren't the only ways to create target markets. Don't worry if you've chosen to do it differently. The important thing is to create groupings based on similar characteristics so you can focus your approach and message to them.

Beware Trees Growing into Mega-Forests

Early in my career I limited my segments only to companies in similar industries regardless of size. In hopes of more prospects, I started with long lists of companies in each group. I learned the hard way that this didn't work!

I discovered that if I referenced a big company like Microsoft in my initial message to small companies, they immediately thought they were too small for us to assist effectively. If I referenced a small company, large prospects thought we were too small to service them. Prospects quickly eliminated us from working with them because they couldn't relate to my reference. Now I always make sure my target market includes companies of similar size so my message relates to them. This is the second cut I use in my own target market definition.

Be careful that your target markets don't grow too large like mine did. Your goal is to create micro-groups of 25–150 companies. Any larger and you'll find your message gets lost like mine did, or you have too many leads to manage while balancing your selling activities. The last thing you want is to attract all these great contacts and then ignore them.

Use multiple characteristics to create micro-segments within your target markets. For example, I use industry, company size, region, and title. This gives me four different cuts and results in very comfortable group sizes and nicely personalized messages.

Keep Your Focus

Focus. It allows you to stop the random prospecting activities that produce weak results. It starts to build name recognition for you in markets where you have strong offerings. It leads you to success.

While you may split your contact base into five or six target markets, I recommend you choose no more than two to focus on at first. Just as you'll begin with only a few attraction strategies, start with two segments.

Choose the ones where you already have:

- Experience selling
- Testimonials and references

- Quantifiable results you can quote

The objective is to choose groups where you'll realize rapid success from your attraction strategies and quickly fill your pipeline.

But in the back of your mind you're concerned about all those other prospects, the ones you're not concentrating on, aren't you? There might be someone in one of your other target markets who has a challenge you can solve. You feel as if you should be working them, too. I understand!

If opportunities outside your segment seek you out, sell to them of course. I'm simply guiding you to concentrate your prospecting efforts within your top two target markets so you can be most effective. Don't worry about the others for now.

Over time, you'll reach out to more of your groups. As you make yourself known, build successes in the first two, and start engaging new companies, you can begin attraction strategies in your next hot segment.

Your focus will pay off by drawing in new contacts as they become more aware of you, notice your message, and recognize that they have a need with which you can assist.

4

Get Your Grabber

．．．．．．．．．．．．．．．．．．．

I love the word "grabber" because it's so descriptive.

When I think about grabbing a prospect's attention, I picture a hook reaching out and catching the contact by surprise. It's not a bad hook. It just makes him stop in his tracks, pause for a moment, and think.

In my mind's eye I picture the prospect looking out the window up at the sky and wondering to himself about what he read or heard. He quickly jots down a note to call me, dashes off an email with his initial thoughts for someone to follow up, or jumps on the Internet to check out an item I recommended.

For that split second, I caught his attention and made him think deeply about what I communicated. It was so compelling that he took immediate action.

That's your objective with your prospect attraction strategies. So how do you grab your contacts' attention and get them to respond to you?

No more creating needs where none exist. It takes too long and is too risky when you have a pipeline to fill. Choose topics they're already concerned about, issues they know they have to deal with, or changes in their business they know they want to make.

Focus on issues that are already top of mind with them.

Use Trigger Events to Trigger a Response

Trigger events are those changes in your target market's companies, community, or world that'll cause your prospects to make an adjustment and possibly a buying decision. It could be as significant as a soft economy where people are being laid off or as minor as frustrating computer outages typical to their industry.

One computer services provider I work with targets accounting firms with 5–50 accountants. My client knows that when an accounting firm's computers are down, it directly impacts productivity, customer satisfaction, and ultimately, revenue. My client also knows that firms this size typically do not have an IT person on staff to fix the problem. It's frequently left to the office manager to address. Long delays and costly repair bills result.

When they happen, computer outages become a trigger event and a tremendous opportunity for my client. It's not as big as the inauguration of a new president or a merger between two organizations, but it impacts accounting firms nonetheless and it creates an opening.

With this in mind, my client created a series of attraction strategies targeting accounting firms frustrated by computer outages. Not every firm the client approached was affected, but those that were expressed interest in learning more about how they could alleviate the issue.

This event wasn't anything you'd find in the newspaper or splashed across the Internet. However, you may choose a headliner because of the impact on your segment and how your offerings can help.

For example, when HIPAA was established it caused a significant change in business processes for all medical professionals from hospitals to single doctors' offices. Companies needed help with everything from records scanning and data security to training their receptionists how to sign patients in differently. Insurance companies required medical offices to use different systems. New forms were necessary for patient processing. Higher levels of security were required to protect patient processing. HIPAA was a compelling trigger event for many medical offices and the sellers supporting them.

Whatever the reason, trigger events are those where you have services to help if:

- You catch prospects when the event is top of mind

- Your reason for contacting prospects is positioned to remind them of the event

Create a Conversation Starter

Trigger events become the topic of everything you do in your target market to attract new prospects.

They aren't necessarily your main subject once you're engaged in the sales process and conducting requirements-gathering discussions. At that point you may find that the trigger event isn't the most significant issue to deal with. However, to grab new contacts' attention all your attraction "conversations" should relate to a trigger event that you've identified as critical to that group. They become your conversation starter.

One trigger event managed services providers frequently experience is a plethora of sales opportunities lingering in the funnel without closing. This segment often focuses on small and mid-size companies who are very cost-conscious. Their customers examine investments from all angles before making a purchasing decision. The managed services providers need to be able to show their prospects how committing to their offerings will help the bottom line right now.

With this challenge in mind, the topic of all my articles, blog posts, emails, and events to managed service providers centers on the number of opportunities stuck in their sales funnels and what to do about it.

The objective is to grab your target market's attention and trigger a discussion about how to address the problem. Once your prospects engage, you're in the sales process. The dialogue may shift from there, but that's okay. You've gained access and we're talking.

You want to do the same with trigger events facing your target market. Pick a few key issues. Talk and write about them everywhere your group will be to hear you.

Uncover Your Target Market's Grabber

Determining the grabber trigger event to use is often easier than you think. Start by looking at the problems your customers faced in their businesses before you began working together.

- What changed in their businesses as a result of working with you?
- How did your solutions help them?
- How did their companies, people, processes, or products improve?

Identify the issues you helped address. My client who works with accounting firms realized that he helped improve their staff productivity when the computer system outages went away. His customers told him they'd seen a direct impact on their overtime costs and employee satisfaction. It was this information that helped him choose computer failure as a trigger event.

Examine your target group and ask yourself:

- What are they talking about?
- What's worrying them?
- What's hindering their productivity that you could help with?
- What are they spending too much on that they don't need to?
- Where could they increase revenues?
- Where are their business processes bogged down?
- What are their competitors doing that they aren't, but should be?

- What's happening in the world around their
  business that can help or hurt them?

Figure out what's causing these problems. The root cause is the trigger event you're looking for. Be sure to choose trigger events and issues your solutions can address.

With these challenges in mind, go one step further and think about how your segment feels when an event occurs. My client's accounting firm customers were experiencing lost productivity because of system outages. That downtime *frustrated* partners, employees, and clients.

A good grabber will evoke strong feelings tied to a memory. It's those strong feelings that cause prospects to immediately pick up the phone and call you. They want to avoid feeling that way again and you can help.

Some excellent emotion-inducing words include:

• Annoyed	• Frustrated	• Confined
• Constrained	• Limited	• Afraid
• Struggling	• Confused	• Discouraged
• Disappointed	• Concerned	• Restricted

Bring the feelings back to the forefront of your target market and you'll grab their attention!

Quote Positive Results for Credibility

As you do your research to uncover the ideal trigger events, listen, too, for the positive results your clients achieved by eliminating the issue. Quoting quantifiable results increases your credibility with prospects who don't yet know you. Specific numbers immediately make you the expert people will want to talk with.

One company I worked with didn't believe in cold calling. The client felt it wasn't appropriate to their target prospects. At the same time, new business development was critical to their growth strategy. They determined that the only way to meet their growth goals was through referrals and engaged us to help them put a referral program in place across the company.

Within seven weeks the organization had increased its number of referrals into new prospects by 328%. These were outstanding results!

That 328% immediately became the results number we used for all our attraction strategies related to new business development. We weaved the number into examples in events and articles, on blog posts, and in prospecting emails. It's included in my social network profiles.

The moment I quote it, people stop to listen, reply to emails, read the articles I send, attend events, watch me on LinkedIn and Twitter, and ask how they can achieve similar results.

The trigger event grabs them. The results solidify their desire to follow up with us.

Consider the benefit you and your company can bring in solving the issue the trigger event is causing for your target market. Ideally the benefit includes measurable value or the return on investment that your prospect can anticipate by addressing the identified challenge.

• Reduce (name the type) costs by x%	• Increase revenue (from where) by y%
• Improve (name whose) productivity	• Reduce time to market
• Improve operational efficiency	• Decrease turnover
• Maximize use of existing technology	• Improve customer satisfaction
• Reduce time to productivity	• Achieve profitability targets
• Acquire more profitable customers	• Ensure compliance with government regulations

Stories Are Great, Too

If you don't have quantifiable results you can mention, not to worry. Use testimonials.

It can be difficult to get clients to measure the impact of your work together. Ask them to tell you in less specific terms what value they believe they have received. Use those quotes as your results without the specific percentages.

You may be pleasantly surprised to find that contacts provide a measurable number you can quote as they start talking about the benefits you've brought to their business. Once they give it to you, bingo! You have quantifiable numbers you can reference. And if they don't, you still have some excellent stories to weave into your attraction strategies.

Keep Two Additional Trigger Events Handy

While you may choose to center your attraction strategies on one key trigger event, have two others top of mind. This adds variety in your communications. It also keeps you flexible in the event that something shifts in your target market.

Alternating different trigger events will keep your attraction strategies fresh and interesting to your whole target market. If one trigger event doesn't hit the mark, another might. People won't get bored and will begin to follow you as an expert who understands them from a broad perspective.

You've grabbed them!

5

Connect Your Efforts

· · · · · · · · · · · · · · · · · · · ·

Right now you're probably thinking, "But Kendra, I've done a lot of these things and prospects still aren't calling me. I've identified my target markets, figured out the trigger events, secured some testimonials, and perhaps even locked in some quantifiable results. Contacts just don't respond to me. Maybe my situation is different than yours?"

It could be, but there's one more trick you need to know. And this one is the hardest of all because it requires planning and execution. That's something we sellers don't always excel at when it comes to prospecting.

We'd prefer to be spontaneous.

Yes, we'll use our customer relationship manager (CRM) software to remind us when to call people already in the sales cycle and to check in on customers. But prospecting is one of those tasks better left for tomorrow.

Then tomorrow never comes. We close all our deals. The funnel dries up. And darn it all there's nothing left to sell.

We have Prospecting Interruptus. It's an illness common to most sellers where we find all the other things we have to do except generating new leads. Unfortunately it strikes hardest on weekday mornings exactly when we're planning our day.

Weekday evenings, typically on a Thursday or Friday, it seems to subside as we take a closer look at the pipeline, panic, then realize we've avoided any prospecting activities all week. We arrive the next day with the best of intentions, but Prospecting Interruptus returns in full force.

It's like a lingering cold. One minute you think you're better. An hour later, you've got it worse than before, focusing on current opportunities with no time to attend to finding new contacts.

The good news is that there's a cure.

Remember, we aren't going to cold call anymore. We aren't talking about picking up the phone to try to reach our target market. We're going to use attraction strategies that bring new contacts to us because they want our help. They're easier, more fun, and much more productive.

The secret to curing Prospecting Interruptus and getting the leads you're looking for is to use the Attraction Trifecta and connect your attraction strategies.

What's Different Now

The difference between what you're doing now and what you've tried in the past is how you'll execute the attraction strategies.

In the past, while you may have sent prospecting emails or forwarded an interesting article, you probably did it as a one-time event. You followed up once, perhaps twice, but that's as far as you went because other priorities took over.

Remember: To hook prospects into coming to you they have to know you, respect you as an expert, and have a reason to talk with you. An occasional email or event isn't going to create awareness for you or your company. It won't establish your credibility or leave a lasting impression. Contacts won't think to call you when they have a problem.

You need a focused approach that continually reminds your target market that you're out there, an expert who understands the issues they're facing and has solutions to help.

When members of your target group suddenly experience the trigger event you've highlighted, or think you can help as an expert, they'll contact you.

Create a Campaign

The way you accomplish this is by simply connecting your attraction strategies, where your segment repeatedly sees and hears about you over a period of time. Without realizing it, you're everywhere they look.

I call this continued level of exposure a campaign. Think about a political campaign. Everywhere you turn for months on end, all you see are candidates telling you how great they are, making promises to alleviate the pain of the day. This is the strategy you want to apply, too.

You deliberately plan a series of prospecting emails, an event, updates to your LinkedIn profile, and blogs to post to. Every few weeks contacts receive an email. If you're connected via a social network, they see updates about you. They read an article or blog in newsletters and on sites they follow.

It's not accidental. You planned it very precisely over a period of time.

Keith, a seller targeting mid-size manufacturers, planned what at first looked like a very elaborate campaign. But when broken down, it actually was a simple formula integrating email, web-based events, blog posts, and social networking, where email was the primary attraction strategy. His trigger event was reduction of budgets to contain rising manufacturing costs. Keith found that many of his clients were very focused on streamlining their processes to reduce costs and meet budget constraints. He sells a technology solution that helps accomplish this.

Here is how the campaign worked:

1. Keith launched his campaign with an email that included two follow-up emails confirming receipt of the initial one. He used the trigger event and quantifiable results to grab attention, then offered a link to a best practice article or the opportunity to discuss the issue by phone.

2. Three weeks later he sent an email invitation to a 50-minute webcast event. The topic was the trigger event, how other clients have addressed it, and results they realized. He sent three additional email invitations to people who had not yet enrolled.

3. After the event he sent a follow-up email to people who either didn't attend or didn't enroll. In it he highlighted key information from the webcast. He included a link to the event recording and offered the opportunity to talk by phone.

Keith's Campaign

Trigger event email campaign   Event invitation   Event   Follow-up

Simultaneously to the email and event strategies, Keith answered questions once a week on two blogs he'd identified that these manufacturers follow. He also updated his social network profiles to highlight that he was helping manufacturers with the trigger event.

The entire campaign spanned four months but only required:

- Creating three main emails with brief follow-up emails to each one

- Producing a webcast event, developed and delivered by a technical support consultant and alliance partner

- Monitoring two blogs weekly for interesting questions to answer

- Writing quick one-sentence weekly updates to his social network profiles

Expect To Be Surprised

Keith was stunned when he began receiving replies with the very first email series. He thought he wouldn't see any leads until after the event. His group only had 75 people in it—all within companies he'd never contacted.

Needless to say, I wasn't surprised because he'd done everything right.

He sent the first email focused on a hot trigger event with
strong quantifiable results. He followed up the first email, not
once but twice. That alerted contacts that it wasn't just another
marketing email. There was a real person behind the emails,
someone who wanted to connect with them.

But he didn't stop with just three emails. He invited contacts to a webcast and followed up on it, too. In addition, he
was visible on the blogs they were reading.

As Keith's campaign progressed, the number of responses
increased. Overall he heard from 39 people in his target
market, either expressing interest or sharing that the timing
wasn't right just yet and asking to stay in touch. More than
52% of his micro-segment responded!

In just four months his integrated campaign that used only
four easy attraction strategies caught manufacturers' attention,
elevating him to expert level.

Take the Next Step

Now that Keith has begun to establish his expertise with his
target market, he doesn't want to let it drop. He can't afford to
allow Prospecting Interruptus to take over or he'll risk losing
the advantage he's created for himself in his segment.

Once your target market becomes aware of who you are
you'll want to continue your attraction strategies but shift to
different approaches.

In the beginning, when members of the group don't know
you, it's important to be visible, building your name directly
with them. Then you can use attraction strategies that will

keep you in front of them but that won't feel too onerous to you or as if you're pestering them.

Another seller I was working with was using email as her primary attraction strategy. Her target market included just 40 contacts. She feared that if she ran a three-month campaign on email alone, her prospects would feel as if she was hounding them. She wasn't comfortable at all until we added a few other simple attraction strategies to keep her in front of her target contacts without always sending a personalized email.

As you plan your campaign, you absolutely want to find prospects who need your services right now. Email, webcasts, follow-up calls, social networking, and speaking are excellent avenues to do this.

At the same time, you want to use attraction strategies that will keep you visible without pushing yourself into your contacts' faces. Blogs, articles, podcasts, social media, and e-newsletters accomplish this nicely for you.

You Can Do This, Too

So about now you're thinking this all sounds pretty time-consuming and you're feeling overwhelmed again. I understand!

If you get real excited, trying lots of different attraction strategies to multiple target markets all at once, it could absorb all your attention. However, you don't need to take a lot of time to create a campaign. Remember, choose only two target markets to get started and a few attraction strategies that feel most comfortable to you.

The top two causes of Prospect Interruptus are:

1. Difficulty
2. Fear

If you start with approaches that are familiar, they'll be easier and more fun for you to implement.

Begin with a 6-to-12 week campaign. A short one will be less complex. You'll see results in six weeks just as Keith did. Over time, you can lengthen your campaigns if you want.

I tend to limit my own campaigns to six weeks to avoid unnecessary complexity. I'll run a campaign targeting individual prospects using email, follow-up calls, and webcasts; then let it rest for four weeks. While it's resting I'm answering blog questions, writing an article, and sending a newsletter to stay visible. After a month, I begin a new targeted campaign.

I give you permission to run a short campaign. The key is to begin. You'll be amazed by the prospects you can attract in only six weeks!

Help! I Need a Plan!

Effective attraction strategies require careful planning. Just as a well-laid-out political campaign is backed by a detailed project plan, so should your attraction campaign have a well thought-out strategy with each critical step documented.

That's not something we as sellers always like to do, but it will help you manage timely execution and thereby increase your results significantly.

Perhaps one of the biggest benefits is that once planned, you can reuse a campaign simply by changing minor messages. I've created a set of prospecting emails that I use across multiple target markets simply by adjusting the trigger event and results. The same can be done with other attraction strategies. It's a great time-saver!

Sales Magnet Tools for You

If you'd like some help with your campaign planning, download The Campaign Planner in the Sales Magnet Tool Kit. It will guide you through key questions to ask yourself to ensure you stay focused on your lead generation goal for the campaign.

6

Make an Offer
They Can't Refuse

think free stuff is great, don't you? I can't resist a free podcast or an e-book on the latest sales strategy, or the opportunity to join a group of peers to discuss industry direction.

Personally, you can keep the silly hats and logo-emblazoned T-shirts. My kids love the clicker pens that pop open and closed, but give me an invitation to a free webcast on a pertinent topic and you've got my attention.

Your prospects love free stuff; too, especially when it'll help clarify their business strategy, solidify an issue they're dealing with, or run their companies more successfully. In a flash you can catch their attention and make them notice you by offering something they perceive to be of value.

That's what offers do for you.

How to Use Offers

Your whole purpose in using attraction strategies is to find new contacts who're interested in working with you. In each strategy you execute, include an offer that'll catch the recipients' attention if they're even remotely interested in the issue you've highlighted.

As you send an email campaign, make an offer to click through to an informational e-book or an educational podcast discussing the trigger event you mentioned or a case study highlighting how a company experienced extraordinary results.

In a webinar you might recommend a free electronic tool to evaluate their situation, the option to sign up for your company newsletter, and the chance to say "I'm interested in learning more about your services."

It's not enough to get prospects' attention. You want to be sure the people who request the offer truly have an interest in the issue at hand. The best way to do that is by making the offer one that'll demonstrate their level of desire if they accept.

When I speak on how to help technical specialists learn to sell, I frequently offer a downloadable assessment that managers complete to determine how their techies' sales ability measures up. Not all companies choose to download it, even though it's free. Those people who enroll and attend but don't download it aren't qualified prospects. They have some interest, but not enough that they want to determine the readiness of their staff to sell. This is a signal that they haven't progressed far enough in their needs analysis just yet. They need to do some additional thinking before they'll be ready to engage in a deeper discussion.

Those participants who do request the tool, however, are pre-qualified. They've taken another step closer to teaching their techies to sell. They most likely would welcome a conversation about their situation and how to address it.

Your objective is to extend offers that are of value to your prospects while helping you quickly distinguish between pre-qualified prospects and merely interested suspects.

Make It Compelling

Your offer shouldn't be a trinket such as a fidget toy for your desk or a T-shirt. Leave those for the trade shows.

You want to choose an offer that prospects in your target market will jump at because it:

1. Focuses on an issue or trigger event they're grappling with.
2. Guides their thinking in a new, strategic direction they're already pondering.

Now, if you have a marketing background, you'll probably add a lot more criteria to the list. That's okay. For those of you who are sellers, your goal is to get prospects to respond to the offer so we can get a conversation started and move new prospects into the sales pipeline.

These two criteria are enough to help pre-qualify if the contact has a need before you call and begin the sales process.

Offers that meet one of these two criteria will be compelling enough to catch the attention of anyone who has the need you're focused on in your attraction campaign.

Educate Your Target Market

Many of the most successful offers are educational and informational in nature. They help prospects:

- Better understand the trigger event
- Evaluate their situation on their own
- Determine their next step in addressing the trigger event

Use your offers to guide contacts through their buying process up to the point that they realize on their own that they need to address the trigger event. Extend offers that allow prospects to learn at their own pace. As they accept your educational offers, prospects realize they could use your assistance. When this realization occurs, prospects appreciate your suggestion to meet and analyze their situation or to see a demonstration.

Nurture Through Offers

Proper staging of your offers allows you to nurture prospects through their buying process. Through your attraction strategies you suggest the type of informational material that helps guide them through learning.

At the beginning of your attraction campaign, extend educational offers that broaden prospects' understanding of the trigger event. Articles and blog posts are helpful here. They're quick to read yet foster deep thought.

As your campaign progresses, provide offers that allow prospects to assess their situation. Podcasts and webcast can detail a situation and highlight possibilities of what business could be like if the trigger event were addressed. On-line assessments and checklists allow prospects to stealthily evaluate themselves and the need for change.

At the end of your attraction campaign, extend the offer to assist with a free analysis, phone discussion, or demonstration.

Use offers to subtly move your interested clients from nominal interest in addressing a trigger event to the desire to speak with you. As your clients request offers to evaluate their situation and determine their next step, they pre-qualify themselves to you.

Easy Offers You Can Make

Today many offers are items that can be downloaded rather than sent through the mail. However don't minimize the value of a pair of colorfully printed tickets to a product launch party or a paperback book that's nicely bound with a handwritten note on personalized stationary. Sometimes receiving a gift through the mail is just as valued.

Your offers should be something free but with perceived value. You're extending them to a target market that may never have heard of you before, so you can't expect them to pay. The offers also have to relate to the issue you're highlighting in your prospect attraction strategy, i.e. cutting overhead costs, reducing hiring expenditures, improving staff productivity.

These are examples of offers that already may be available to you for different sales purposes. It just requires thinking about them from a different perspective—as special, prized offers, not just sales collateral.

Educational offers from your company library:

- A podcast or webcast recording
- An e-book, blog post, book or article
- A tip sheet, such as *Top 10 PowerProspecting Tips*
- A technical white paper or case study
- An on-line checklist of assessment
- An invitation to attend a webcast, teleseminar, trade show, or other event
- An electronic tool, such as a *Customer Service ROI Analysis* or a set of templates
- A chapter from a user manual

Informational offers from your networking and on-going research:

- A link to an appealing blog post
- An invitation to link to a group of interest on a social network
- An introduction to a well-known peer in the industry

Offers already part of your sales process:

- An idea to help grow their business or address an issue
- A free analysis or assessment
- A personal visit to offer recommendations in line with their requirements
- A quick phone discussion about their situation and how you've seen others handle similar ones
- A trial or demonstration
- A meeting with a top visiting executive

Leverage Other Experts for Offers

Many sellers have the opportunity to leverage offers from outside their organization, too. If you don't have a wide base of material to pull from within your own company, never fear. If you resell another company's products as part of your solutions, that company may have offers you can use.

One group we work with sells telecommunication solutions that run on Microsoft servers. Every installation or upgrade to a client's system also includes Microsoft software. And Microsoft is more than happy to provide any type of offer that will help drive additional leads to our client because of the potential revenue it represents.

Your alliance partner doesn't have to be a Fortune 500 behemoth to have educational offers you can leverage. Look at what offers the partner uses in its lead generation activities and the resources it makes available. Ask to include those resources and offers in your prospect attraction strategies.

No alliance partners? There's still no reason to panic!

The Internet is chock full of information that people have placed there for others to find and use. That means you can capitalize on it as well. Some items to consider using:

- Articles, e-books, and blog posts
- Research reports and papers
- Recordings, YouTube videos
- Tip sheets

Provide a link to them and be sure to give credit to the author.

Don't attempt to claim these offers as your own works. Rather, position yourself as the expert who has found this valuable information and wants to bring it their attention. Your prospects will appreciate that you did and remember you as a thought leader.

Close the Deal with a Call to Action

Every attraction strategy you use should encourage prospects to respond to you immediately. As in selling you must close the deal. To accomplish this, include a call to action in each one.

A call to action is the request you make of your prospect to do something. It tells him exactly what you want him to do when he's done. For example:

- Use this link to download the tip sheet.
- Listen to this podcast.
- Click and read this article.
- Enroll in the webcast.
- Call me if you'd like to brainstorm ideas about . . .
- Sign up your team.
- Forward this to . . .
- Call to set an appointment.
- Dial in and listen.
- If you have immediate questions, call me or email me at . . .

Even a holiday card has an implied call to action: Please take my call the next time I phone you because I took the time to send you a nice card!

It isn't enough to assume your prospects will know what they're supposed to do. Tell them precisely what you want from them using simple, succinct language. Go beyond just including a link and expecting them to realize that they should click through. Close the deal with: "Use this link to download the *Top 10 PowerProspecting Tips.*"

You might choose to have prospects provide information before accessing the offer. In this case, ask for as minimal an amount as possible. The goal is for interested prospects to receive the offer and you to be informed. You don't need to know their full mailing address, number of people in the company, and three phone numbers. The more information you require, the less comfortable prospects will be in providing it. They may choose to pass on the offer and you'll lose your lead. Think carefully about the level of detail that's truly necessary.

When a person accepts your call to action, it signifies an interest, prequalifying him. If the prospect doesn't respond, you'll need to find another way to reach him. It doesn't mean he's not qualified, only that your attraction approach or offer didn't catch his attention.

Without the call to action, you've wasted your opportunity to close the deal and generate a lead.

Make it Easy to Reach You

Now that you've caught your prospects' attention with a compelling offer and told them what to do, make it as easy as possible to reach you if they have an immediate need.

In every attraction strategy make it your goal to offer three ways to respond. You don't necessarily need to include it in the body of an email, social media comment, or blog, but find a way to incorporate this in case they want to connect.

For instance, in a webcast you're running, end with a slide that offers at least three ways to reach you. If you're writing an article, include your email, phone number, and website in your article bio at the bottom. When blogging or answering a discussion question, include a way to contact you at the end of each post. For social media comments, be sure your key contact information is obviously visible in your profile and accept direct messages.

Why three ways? Because everyone is different.

When it's urgent, your prospects want to know they can reach you right now—and that typically means a phone call. If they're busy, they may prefer to dash off an email and start the ball rolling. If they want to do a bit more exploration and watch you, Twitter or LinkedIn might be their best fit. And if they'd like to see if you have what they're looking for, they may prefer to jump right to your website.

In today's electronic age you can offer many more than three connection opportunities. Consider any of the following but always include your phone number and email address:

- Direct link to your LinkedIn, Facebook, Twitter or other social media profiles
- Skype
- Website or blog
- Your assistant
- An inside sales rep
- Customer support
- An alliance partner

Many sellers worry that this type of flagrant promotion of their contact information will cause unwanted SPAM or unsolicited sales calls to them. You might see an increase in both, but with the sophisticated SPAM-blocking software available today, it's easy to avoid those emails. And with so few sellers actually cold calling anymore, you're likely to see few of them coming your way.

Ensure that everywhere your prospects encounter you there are at least three ways for them to get in touch with you. Make it simple to reach you when the time is right and you'll find that you are attracting more hot prospects than you expected. No cold calling required.

Sales Magnet Tools for You

To see an example of an informative, educational offer we use, take a look at the *Top 10 PowerProspecting Tips* in the Sales Magnet Tool Kit. You'll notice that it's a quick read for people with simple, actionable tips they may have forgotten or never considered. Executives can share it with their sales teams and sellers appreciate it for themselves, so it's appropriate for different contacts within a target market, making it a very versatile offer.

Part 2

Pick Your Personal
Attraction Strategies

By now your coffee is probably drained and you have a good idea how to set yourself up for a barrage of new prospects using target markets, linked campaigns, a grabber to catch their attention, and an offer they can't refuse.

Choose a Few Prospect Attraction Strategies

The next step is to choose a few prospect attraction strategies from the Attraction Trifecta and apply some of the techniques you've learned so far. Within the Attraction Trifecta there are 14 approaches you can use to get more prospects. The objective is to pick those approaches that feel most comfortable to you.

Personal

Digital

Collaborative

While ordinarily you'd like to stretch yourself and grow, your goal is to get more prospects. That means you need to choose strategies that easily fit your selling style. Over time you can expand and try different attraction strategies, but for now let's go with what will work best for you.

Your Guide to Success

The chapters in the next three sections include personal, digital and collaborative activities you can do as a seller to attract prospects. Each chapter delves into:

- how to use the activity.
- what results you can expect.
- special tips and tricks to increase your success ratio.

This is your guide to success.

As you read through the strategies, choose one or two to begin your attraction campaign. You can attract prospects using just one approach if you're diligent in your execution, so don't feel you need to start with a bunch.

Results You Can Expect

Michael, a software sales rep I work with, is busy following up on sales opportunities and supporting existing clients. He doesn't have time to do much prospecting. He's committed to just two personal attraction strategies, email campaigns and phone pursuit. He makes time to launch them every two weeks. He has a steady flow of new prospects who have responded to offers and expressed interest. He's given up cold calling and averages 23 new leads a month.

Carl, a managed services client, is focused on expanding his business regionally. He uses a combination of collaborative and digital attraction strategies as his lead generation approach. He speaks at local and on-line events three times a quarter and uses his articles as offers in his follow-up. He averages 12–15 new leads every time he speaks to his target market at an event.

I've used every one of these approaches and produced leads for myself and our clients with each one, so I can vouch for their effectiveness. Choose the Trifecta attraction strategies that appeal to you; then commit to doing them on a consistent basis. Use the tips and tricks outlined in the next three sections to identify the winning combination most suitable to you and you'll get results.

Personal Attraction Strategies

Personal

Personal attraction strategies are those activities where the prospect feels like you've reached out to make a personal connection. Even though you may be using the example same email or letter content, they can't tell.

With personal attraction strategies you have a list of people you are targeting from your micro-segment. You direct all communications to the contacts on your list. Nobody outside your list will receive your communication unless someone on the list forwards it to them.

This allows you to personalize your content and make it very specific to your target market. It also allows you to conduct a very controlled campaign. You can manage the follow-up activities, like phone calls, in such a manner that you avoid having too many contacts to call at once.

Every successful lead generation campaign I've seen includes at least one personal attraction strategy. That's because at some point you have to reach out and communicate directly with the individuals in your target market to set the first appointment. The personal attraction strategies allow you to do this in an efficient manner, while still feeling personal to your prospects.

There are five personal attraction strategies.

1. **Email**—including prospecting emails and series of emails written as a campaign to reach prospects in a way they can easily reply

2. **Letters**—sent through the postal service, but personalized so they don't feel like a direct mail letter

3. **Post cards and other variations of letters and emails**—including unusual ways you can use postcards and letters to catch prospects' attention

4. **Personal networking**—where you meet prospects in person to uncover leads or build your list of contacts in your target market

5. **Phone pursuit**—using warm calling to increase response rates from your campaigns

Use the tips and tricks in this section to establish a personal connection with prospects in your target market and uncover new leads.

7

Email Prospecting

E mail has replaced cold calling for many sellers. It's less threatening for you and easier for your prospects to respond. As an added bonus, the results from your email campaigns can be quite impressive when they're individualized. With that in mind this is a personal attraction strategy you definitely want to consider including in your lead generation arsenal.

Email has become so popular that there are tons of suggestions available. You can read blogs, white papers, case studies, and more. You want to apply those tips that work for you as a seller. Sure, you can use some of the marketing tips, but your objective is to uncover real prospects with real needs right now.

The tips I'm going to give you in this chapter apply to sellers who're using email as a prospecting tool. They're proven, with many success stories to support them. Perhaps one of my favorites is from Helen, an online subscription software seller who attended an Email PowerProspecting audio conference we did for her company.

Helen had 60 leads that were over six months old and had never progressed. They were sitting in her CRM system and she was struggling with what to do with them. The contacts never had responded to any calls or previous emails. After our program, she decided to change the content of her email and try again. In one day, after just one email, Helen received 43 replies. She received so many that it took her the entire next day to respond to them all.

With some simple adjustments, Helen had a 71.7% response rate!

Now, I know what's in the back of your mind. You're thinking, "But Helen had 60 leads who'd contacted her at some point, so they already knew her. I'm skeptical that I can get that many replies from a cold call email campaign." Read on and I'll share how you can get leads from email prospecting even if your target market doesn't know about you yet.

The Glimpse Factor

In three seconds your prospects make a choice between reading and trashing your email. I call this the Glimpse Factor. Prospects quickly determine if they need to read what you've sent or can let it go without even opening it.

The Glimpse Factor is what a prospect thinks when he first glimpses your message. In their subconscious your contacts are asking themselves three questions with every message you send.

1. Do I have time for whatever it is right now?

2. Can I delete it and do nothing at all?

3. Should I hold on to it and do something later?

These are the three questions prospects ask themselves no matter which prospect attraction strategy you use, however they're most prevalent in email. With this in mind, you need to write not only compelling, personalized messages, but also messages that appear easy to respond to.

Break the Delete Barrier

Clearly your objective is to get prospects not only to read the email but to respond so you can set an appointment and begin the sales process. That means you need to find a way to get past their Glimpse Factor and avoid the delete barrier.

There are two keys to successful email prospecting:

1. The message, both what it says and how it looks in a prospect's email in-box
2. The follow-up

Even if you're emailing a list of prospects who never have heard of you or your company, you can get replies from your campaigns.

Hank, a benefit insurance seller, does all his prospecting through email. He was very discouraged because his emails weren't generating any responses. He followed up with cold calls and discovered that the emails hadn't even been opened.

When we reviewed his emails together we discovered that they were long and arduous, centering primarily on his services and how they've helped other clients. Additionally, he'd sent them on an email template that included a graphic resembling a newsletter banner with bullets and multiple font colors throughout. Nothing felt personal.

Hank's emails needed an extreme makeover to draw his message out and grab his prospects' attention. As Hank changed his approach, he suddenly saw an increase in responses. Within one week, he'd secured an appointment for a $187,000 opportunity with a new company. Email prospecting does work, if you know how to appeal to your contacts.

What follows are tips to use the Glimpse Factor to your advantage, write compelling messages, and create emails that will break your prospects' delete barrier. In the next chapter, we'll show you how to use email follow-up to increase your odds of receiving a response.

Email Prospecting Tips and Tricks

Limit the number you send. Don't send more emails than you can respond to. Helen sent 60 emails and found herself overwhelmed when she immediately received 43 responses. People today expect you to respond to their email within 24 hours. In the back of their minds, though, they're expecting a reply within a couple of hours.

I recommend limiting the number of emails you send to *no more than* 150 contacts at a time. Some prospects will respond immediately and others may take several days. If you're very busy, limit them to between 20 and 25 prospects. If you're looking for a big response quickly, send as many as 150 but be sure you schedule time on your calendar in advance to follow up on all the replies.

Find the right email addresses. This is always the biggest issue for sellers. They secure a list of names for their target market but don't know where to go to get email addresses. While you can send an email to info@prospectcompany.com the odds are against you that your message will ever reach your intended recipient.

Follows are several excellent sources to overcome that hurdle.

1. Look within your own CRM first

   - Newsletter, marketing, or trade show lists

   - Vendor lists you may have received

   - Old prospecting lists that were never called and fall within your target market

2. Leverage free lists

   - Data.com contacts by Jigsaw

   - Netprospex.com

3. Use outside list builders

   - ZoomInfo.com

   - Insideview.com

   - Hoovers.com and Dun & Bradstreet

   - Local Chamber of Commerce lists

4. Check with alliance partners and associations

   - Sometimes alliance partners will share their lists if you're running a joint campaign; if they don't have a list, they may pay for you to purchase one.

   - As an association member, you may receive a member list that includes email addresses

5. Search your social networks

   - LinkedIn

   - Facebook

- Twitter

6. Employ a bit of research

    - Web-based news sources

    - Blogs

    - Job postings with email addresses

If there's a prospect you're trying to reach via email but none of these techniques worked, you may be able to deduce that address by searching other contacts from the same company in your social network. If you can find one or two contact's email addresses, you can probably use that information to figure out what your prospect's address would be.

And of course, you can always call the company to ask. Sometimes receptionists are most helpful and provide contact information!

For a line-up of list-building resources and links, check out the online Sales Magnet Tool Kit.

Tailor your message. With small groups, you can use very specific trigger events to catch prospects' attention. Your message will feel personal to the contact even if it was sent to a group of 50 names. The more customized your message, the better chance you have that they'll feel an obligation to respond to you.

Include the trigger event, emotion-inducing words, and results you've achieved with others clients in your initial emails. Combined, they act as a grabber to pull in your prospect. In follow-up emails, forward the initial email and refer to it. No need to repeat the same information.

Personalize the subject line. The sender and subject line are the first two places your prospects glimpse before determining if they're going to delete or read an email. If you're sending to people who won't recognize your name or your company name, it's critical that the subject line grab their attention and entice them to open it.

Use subject lines that feel personal to the contact, as if you had them top of mind and just this moment decided to connect with them. Some of my favorites are questions or statements that assume the prospect will meet with you and inquire about their availability.

- Can we talk next week?

- Meeting next Tuesday at 2pm

- Can you attend?

Or, you may choose a subject line that intrigues them with an idea but is still professional.

- An idea for reducing your IT operational costs

- A thought about improving response times for customers

- An idea for continuing your critical research in the event of a disaster

What I like about mentioning an idea or thought is that it still feels more relaxed and individual. While a marketing-generated email might say "Reduce Your IT Operational Costs," your email suggests that you've thought about the high cost of maintaining computer systems that Johnson Inc. is grappling with and have an idea you want to share to reduce expenditures. The executive you send it to will definitely open your email to see what new brainstorm you have. You won't disclose the idea in your email because your objective is to set up a meeting. But you will let him or her know you have one and would like to share it with them when you talk.

As a word of caution, avoid subject lines that are gimmicky. They're fun to write but are often the first ones to hit the delete barrier. Instead, keep them related them to the body of your email.

Use a salutation. It's very unusual to find an email in North America, Europe, or Australia that is addressed to the person's surname (Hi Mr. Simpson). Remember, your strategy is to be more informal. Begin prospecting emails with the contact's first name, for example:

Tom,

Hi Jeff,

Dear Sally,

Good morning Andrea,

If you don't have a name, eliminate the company from your list until you secure one. Sending an email with no name will immediately hit the delete barrier and destroys your image of writing directly to your prospect.

Invite them in with your signature. Your signature line is an excellent way to invite prospects to get to know you, and you want to leverage it. With the amount of social networking information available today, include a link to one of your publically available profiles, such as LinkedIn or Facebook. If you use Twitter or Skype, include your ID.

Promote your company by including a tagline promoting what you do, an upcoming event, a new podcast, YouTube video, or recent article.

Each of these links is an opportunity for your prospect to click through and learn more about you, making them more comfortable about reaching out to you. They increase your credibility and help you establish a connection before you've even met.

If you do business internationally, you can subtly advertise it by including your country code with your phone number. Large prospects will recognize the significance, providing you instant credibility with them.

Below is an example of my initial email signature. It includes all my contact information as well as links to social network profiles. The tagline at the bottom makes an educational offer.

Best regards,

Kendra

President | Phone: +1 303.741.6636 | E-mail: kendra.lee@klagroup.com | www.klagroup.com KLA Group, LLC
View my LinkedIn profile at http://www.linkedin.com/in/kendralee

Twitter: twitter.com/KendraLeeKLA | Facebook: www.facebook.com/KLAGroup

Prospecting a pain? Download your free copy of our new PowerProspecting Sales Kit

---

This is the signature I use for lead generation and prospecting emails that I initiate. My reply email is shortened slightly but still includes contact information and a tagline.

Keep them short. Keep your initial email as brief as possible to ensure it's at least skimmed. Ideally, you want your prospects to read the complete email, which means you need to make it a quick read. Include a trigger event at the beginning that the majority of your target market can relate to, drawing them in immediately, and then get to your point.

As a rule, include no more than four sentences in a paragraph. If possible, limit your email to three paragraphs plus a one-line sentence as your closing paragraph.

Insert a one-line paragraph in the middle to make it appear short.

Forget what your seventh grade English teacher said. Emails must feel personal and less formal than a business letter. Throw away the perfect grammar and write conversationally. The more comfortable your email, the more likely you'll get a response.

Here are the new rules:

- Use conjunctions.

- End sentences with a preposition if appropriate.

- Include a one-sentence paragraph that fosters a fast read.

- Don't worry if one thought carries across two paragraphs.

- Don't spell out numbers.

- Abbreviate days of the week, typical industry terms (such as IT), and commonly abbreviated words like "info."

Limit the number of links. Just as in cold calling, your objective in email prospecting is to secure an appointment to start a discussion. Some sellers get so excited about what they sell that they include a bunch of links in the body of their email to tell their story. They think it'll excite prospects and make them want to engage in a conversation. In actuality, the more information you give away in your email, the less need your prospects have to speak with you to determine if they should be working with you.

Hold back all your great stuff until you've talked to your prospects and identified what information to send.

Focus on the trigger event and results you can bring. Include a link to your educational offer, but nothing more. No attachments. No white papers. Just the offer related to the trigger event.

The added benefit of just one link is that you appear less like a marketing newsletter and more like a real person. Your prospects are more inclined to read your text than delete it.

Give prospects multiple ways to respond. Even though prospects can simply hit "reply" to respond to you, they may be eager to talk to you right away. Be sure you give them the option of calling you, connecting on LinkedIn, following you on Twitter, and reaching out to you in any other way convenient for them.

Your signature will include your social network information and phone number, and I recommend including your phone number in the body of your email as well. Not everybody will scroll down to the bottom of your email to find it. If your phone number is written in the body of your email with your call to action, your contacts will read it as part of the email and see it as an additional way to easily contact you.

Avoid spam traps. Spam blocking is an issue with every email you send to people you don't know, and even with some prospects who've invited you to contact them. Here are six tips to help you glide past spam traps:

1. Avoid using banners or signatures with graphics. These are often flagged as spam by the system and blocked.

2. Limit the number of links to one in the body of the email and three or four in your signature.

3. Use a company email address rather than a
   general "gmail," "yahoo" or other public email
   system address.

4. Avoid sending from a generic company email
   address such as "sales@" or "info@."

5. Be careful to keep your subject business-related
   and not sales-oriented.

6. Don't send individual emails to a large number
   of people within the same company at the same
   time with the same subject line. Often when you
   do this the email is flagged as spam and even
   the people who have white-listed your email
   address won't receive it. Vary your subject line
   and the time you send the emails so they enter
   the prospect company's email server at different
   times.

When to Avoid Email

There are two situations when you would want to avoid email.

1. Your target market doesn't use email.

2. You can't get a good list of your target market's
   email addresses, or it would take you a long time
   to clean up a list.

A word about email permission laws. If you want to
email a large list and you're not targeting the message of your
emails, you need to be aware of permission laws surrounding email campaigns. In many countries it's against the law to

send emails without the recipient's agreement. In those cases, you can't email unless you can find a way to make the message completely targeted to your prospects so it applies directly to them or you have their permission to email them.

The easiest way to ensure you have permission is to purchase a list from a company that's already done it for you. Companies like ZoomInfo have an internal process to secure authorization before they make email addresses available to their customers.

Another strategy is to get approval through a different lead-generation activity. For example, Tom delivered a webcast on *Leveraging Open Source Tools in Your Business*. He offered a checklist of ways to leverage the tools with a call to action to sign up for an electronic newsletter. All the people who responded positively gave Tom permission to email them.

If you don't use a lead generation activity to get permission, your email must be specifically personalized to your prospect. It can still have a call to action. However, if it appears to be an advertisement, you risk it being screened as spam, deleted immediately, responded to angrily with a "REMOVE" in the subject line, or reported as breaking the law. If any one of these occurs, you have lost the potential lead, possibly lost all permission to email the contact, may lose permission to send emails through your email hosting company, and may even have a legal battle on your hands.

To avoid any of these negative responses, be sure your emails have a message that relates directly to your contact.

Despite the fear of legal action, email is one of the most effective ways to reach your prospects today. Done right, they'll take notice of your messages and respond when they have a need.

Sales Magnet Tools for You

For more tips and tricks on increasing the effectiveness of your prospecting emails, check out the Email PowerProspecting Sales Kit in the Sales Magnet Tool Kit. You'll also find a line-up of additional email address list-building resources and links.

8

Create an Email Campaign to Increase Results

Once you master writing prospecting emails, it's time to increase your results using a campaign strategy. The campaign strategy is your follow-up approach that keeps you front and center with prospects. Our research shows that a higher percentage of your target market will respond after four emails than only one email. With this in mind, why wouldn't you expand your prospecting emails into campaigns?

Here's how an email campaign works:

1. Prospects hear from you several times over a few weeks.

2. Your emails gradually get more personal. Your prospects realize the emails aren't part of a marketing campaign. Rather, it's a real person who wants to connect with them.

3. Prospects respond.

Here are my top tips and tricks for a successful email campaign.

Email Campaign Tips and Tricks

Email every two days, then rest. The first time you send an email your prospect may not realize it came from a real person who wants to connect with him. But with a personalized message and follow-up strategy, you'll quickly change his mind. (Remember, your personalized message is the one focused on the trigger event you identified for the target market and the results you can provide by addressing the issues behind the trigger event.)

Three days after you've sent your first email, forward it with a new email. Say something like:

> Just wanted to check in to see if we can schedule a time to talk next week per my email below. By chance are you open next Wednesday afternoon or Thursday morning?

> Were you able to read the blog post about levering the stimulus package to convert your medical records to digital? I have some additional ideas for you. How's your schedule next Wednesday for us to talk?

Use this approach to send three additional follow-up emails, changing each one slightly, still forwarding the original one. Send them each three days apart.

Your response rate will increase as people realize that you really want to connect with them.

After four emails, rest your list of contacts that you haven't heard from. Wait two weeks, then email them again with a new trigger event, educational offer, and results message.

Create a set of prepared responses. If you find yourself in Helen's lucky situation with 43 emails all at once, you'll want a set of email replies you can quickly copy and edit.

Create a few general emails before launching the campaign, matching them to the types of answers you expect based on the content of the email you're sending. As you receive replies, tailor the general email to fit with what your prospect wrote.

Queue emails. This my favorite prospecting tip because it solves the problem of following up with prospects in a timely manner.

Often when you finally hear from contacts, they ask you to "call back in a month." The trigger event is important to them, but they just aren't prepared to discuss it yet.

Many sellers log these requests in their CRM system, wait until the appropriate time to check in, and then call or email when the activity pops up. The challenge is that you're often busy with other customer requirements when the prospect's name appears. Suddenly your follow-up slips several days, weeks, or even a month.

To avoid the issue, use the queue feature in your email system. Write your follow-up email as soon as you get off the phone with the prospect while the discussion is top of mind. Then set it up to send in the timeframe he requested. Blind copy yourself as a reminder that the email has been sent. You're on top of the lead without missing a step!

Give yourself time to follow up. People expect a quick response to email. Schedule time on your calendar to follow up as the responses and returns come in *before* you launch the email campaign. Each prospect requires a personalized response; even a three-line email may take five minutes to write. Fifteen responses could take 75 minutes. If each prospect sends a response to your response, that may entail *another* 5–10 minutes of writing time. Be sure you have the time to respond.

Helen got caught when she received 43 responses to her 60 emails. She hadn't planned it into her schedule and found herself working late into the evening to quickly reply to everyone.

Avoid overlapping campaigns. When launching new email campaigns, avoid overlapping a target market where an email campaign is already running. In this instance, your messages from the two campaigns need to be integrated so it appears that you are sitting at your computer writing the email to only your prospect—not to 124 other people. Ideally, you want to combine the emailings from both campaigns into one email message. When you do this, it *does* appear as if you are writing personal emails.

At one point I was running a series of four different email campaigns into the same segment over a six-month period. To avoid sending multiple or conflicting emails, I wrote them so each email contained the messages from the four separate campaigns. The campaigns involved sophisticated tracking of prospect responses in our CRM, as well as different messages for different responses, to successfully run for that length of time. It took a great deal of coordination and planning, but the response rate was phenomenal—nearly 72%, because it appeared as if I were writing to each person individually.

All this is quite complex and you may not have the time to do it. In that case, limit yourself to one campaign per micro-segment.

Following up with email lead generation non-responders. People frequently ask me what to do about all those people who never respond to anything. What it means is that you haven't hit on a trigger event or business issue those people have. When you do, they'll respond.

You may choose to follow up with a phone call, or you could launch another email campaign with a different trigger event. If you emailed a small group, it's easy to do. However, if your group is too large to call, or you don't have the time to do it, rest the list and touch them again with the next campaign. When you hit upon a need they have your prospects will respond.

Integrate email with other activities. Email has become as common as a phone call and often more effective. Integrate email into your other lead generation campaign activities and you'll find it increases your response rate.

Adapt these tips if you're in Marketing.

The tips and tricks I just shared create very personal emails that elicit significant response rates. If you're running marketing email campaigns, some of these suggestions may not be feasible for you. Consider how you can adapt them to your processes, lists, and email systems. Use the suggestions that can work in your situation.

9

Letters with a Personal Touch

The debate is on. Are letters and postcards passé, replaced by email? Do people really read them?

Many sellers believe that old-fashioned mail never gets past the garbage can. But, this form of prospecting can be very effective if your contacts feel it was sent especially for them. Not only do contacts open and read the letters, but if a letter contains valuable information prospects believe they'll use in the future, they'll save your letter!

Carolyn, one sales rep we work with, swears by personal letters as one of her top prospect attraction strategies. She has countless stories of prospects who have saved letters she's sent them, then called six months later when they realized they needed help. Carolyn's prospects aren't in a rural area. They aren't small companies. And yes, they do use email. But when askedher her prospects have explained that when they file a letter in their desk it can often be easier to find than when they file it electronically.

In addition, there are many industries that still don't use email consistently. For example, in some regions, medical and dental practices rarely check email even if they have it. For these industries especially you want to consider sending letters with a personal touch. It may be the only way you can reach these prospects without calling or stopping in their office.

So don't write off using the postal service just yet. When done correctly, it's highly effective and can result in response rates much greater than 5%.

Two Keys to Personal Attraction Strategy Success

The two keys to success in personal activities are that they:

1. Feel as if the activity was directed to the recipient only.

2. Aren't directed to the recipient only.

This is counterintuitive, I know. But if you can successfully make your personal activities feel personal to each prospect, you'll find your physical mail response rates increase.

To accomplish the personalized feel, leverage the similarities of your target market to write one set of letters or postcards highlighting the trigger event, offering something informational and relevant, and making a call to action. Insert a tidbit bit about yourself in the content, then use technology to merge in the names of the contacts from your target market.

To put in yourself in the right frame of mind forget about those marketing direct mail letters you've read. They're long, with multiple colors, bold fonts strategically placed throughout, and pre-printed signatures. They use tired phrases like "special offer" and "select group of people." They don't feel individualized at all and, with one glance, hit the recycling bin.

Instead, think holiday letters, birthday cards, and vacation postcards.

When you review your letter to your micro-segment, it should feel almost like a holiday letter: Friendly, full of relevant news of interest to the recipient, enticing him to want to pick up the phone and connect with you. Your postcards are like a brief note on a birthday card or picture postcard—personal, light, and interesting, drawing the contact closer to you.

These types of letters and postcards create action, connect with prospects, and attract leads.

Get Noticed

With the popularity of email and web-based marketing, fewer companies seem to be using letters as a lead generation strategy. What they don't realize is that a professionally addressed letter can create awareness for your company name, even if it's not opened!

Just as with email, the Glimpse Factor comes into play. In a split second prospects make a decision to read your letter or toss it. Your recipient looks at how the letter is addressed, then speed-reads the return address to see if he recognizes the sender or the company.

Regardless if a prospect has ever heard of your company, when he reads the return address to determine whether to open it, you begin to create awareness. Not many sellers use letters or postcards to attract prospects, and therefore it can be very effective for you, especially when combined with other lead generation activities.

Letter Tips and Tricks

Limit the number you mail. The number one rule of all prospect attraction is to include only as many contacts as you can follow up on.

Based on your campaign strategy, determine what you're capable of in conjunction with your regular selling activities. You might be able to follow up on only 20 letters each week with an email. Or you might choose to set aside a lead generation day on your calendar and call as many as 75 contacts. The campaign strategy you choose dictates the size of your mailing.

Of course, your follow-up capabilities also depend on the method of follow-up you choose to use. If you have an inside sales or telemarketing person you can integrate into your attraction strategy, you can probably mail 125 letters and have your telemarketer call everybody in a matter of a few days. But if the telemarketer sets 20 appointments from these calls, are you prepared to conduct that many within a week or two? If, on the other hand, you are contacting everybody personally, 125 may be too large a number for you to handle. If you are emailing as your next step, mail to only as many people as you can email and then respond to when their replies pile into your inbox.

Before sending out the mailing, schedule your follow-up time on your calendar.

Stagger mailings. Send mailings in small batches, limiting the number of letters to the amount of time you have available.

My rule of thumb is to mail in batches of 20 when my time is tight and in batches of 50 if I'm able to schedule a whole day for follow-up calling.

A follow-up email is easier than calling every contact. Sending a second letter or postcard is easy, too. If, however, at some point in your campaign you have an included an attraction strategy to call everyone who hasn't responded, you must be prepared to meet that commitment.

Give prospects three ways to respond. The challenge with a letter is that prospects must take the time to do something to respond to you. It's not as simple as email where you can hit "reply" and be done. They have to go to another communication tool and do something: Pick up the phone, sign onto the Internet, or log into email.

Your goal is to attract prospects, so make it as easy as possible for them to connect with you, providing a minimum of three ways to respond. The most common today are:

- An email address
- A phone number to reach you directly or leave a voicemail message
- A Web address to request the offer or learn more
- A fax number if appropriate to your industry
- An address where prospects can visit you in your office if suitable

The Web address, office address, and fax number are typically in your letterhead. Be sure to add your email address and direct number in the closing paragraph.

Avoid social media IDs and profile links. While you definitely want to include a link your social network ID in an email signature, it isn't appropriate in a letter. Wait until you've begun establishing a relationship to include it in a letter, and then hand-write it in so it looks like an afterthought.

The one exception to this rule is if the topic of your letter or offer relates to social media. Then it's okay to include it. However, most of the time any offer you make should point them to your website so they can experience the full value of your company.

How to address prospects in a letter. Letters are more formal than email, so your seventh grade English teacher's rules apply. Begin the letter with "Dear." You don't know the person and it's incorrect to jump in with "Hi."

First name or surname? This is a cultural decision. In North America, most of Europe, and Australia, business has become so casual that a letter addressed to Mr. Johnson is automatically screened as direct mail and tossed.

The challenge is when your list informs you that Mr. Johnson's first name is M. Here you have no choice if you want to use a name. You must write Mr. Johnson or find a way to learn what M stands for.

There's also the problem of abbreviating names such as Michael, Robert, and Charles. Don't assume. I know several Michaels that take offense to being called Mike. If you get it wrong, your communication will stand out as an obvious marketing letter and you lose your attraction opportunity.

You need to make a decision on how you want to handle the situation. You have three quick options:

1. Don't mail to this prospect.

2. Use Mr. or Ms. rather than the first name.

3. Do some research to find out the name.

I recommend doing the research. This is your target market and you've honed it to a micro-segment. Take a few minutes to call the company and ask: "I want to send Mr. Johnson a letter and would like to properly address the envelope. Can you tell me if he goes by Michael or prefers a different name?" This approach quickly gives you the answer you need.

One word of caution: If you're calling a small company, be prepared that Mr. Johnson may actually pick up the phone! In this case, be ready to answer the question, "Oh, what are you sending?" As with a cold call, know what you're going to say and turn this into an opportunity to set an appointment.

Closing the letter. Your letter is an opportunity to begin a relationship, so use the closing to facilitate it. The following are traditional closes but won't foster a connection as easily:

- Sincerely

- Regards

- Yours truly (although used less today)

Consider branching out, getting a bit more personal in keeping with your holiday letter, and use a form of these:

- Best regards, or Warm regards
- Warmly
- Looking forward to our discussion
- Looking forward to meeting you

Letter length, bullets, and other rules. Try to limit your letter to three-quarters of one business page, or one full page at a maximum. The Glimpse factor is important to remember when you structure your letter. Make your letter look easy and personal. Here are some specifics on how to accomplish that through your formatting.

- Use an 11 or 12 point font and 1 to 1.5 inch margins on both sides so it's easier to read. Leave the right margin ragged, not justified.

- Limit paragraphs to five sentences but try to vary

paragraph lengths so they look more interesting. Use short paragraphs. Keep in mind that people tend to read the first and last sentence in a paragraph, then decide if they want to read the whole thing. If your paragraph is too long, the meat of it will be left unread.

- Use short sentences. Avoid acronyms or words that may not be easily understood.

- Use short words. Strive for 65–75% of your words being five letters or less.

- Avoid negative words. They convey doubt and uncertainty. Often the phrase "don't" is misread and leaves you sounding like you do something that you really wanted to say you do not do.

- Include bullets. Make sure they are relevant and impactful as they may be the first thing your prospect reads. Use them to draw the reader into the whole letter.

To stamp or meter? Do you meter the birthday cards you send? Probably not. Use a stamp and avoid the meter. There's nothing personal about a metered envelope, and it's the first one to be tossed.

Recipients look at the stamp before they look at who sent the envelope so choose a fun stamp, too.

The U.S. Forever stamps are handy, but choose the interesting ones rather than the more generic Liberty Bell. Don't you buy the pretty stamps for your holiday and birthday cards? Or, wouldn't you like to if you had the time?

Make the time. Your results will show it.

What about Express Mail? This is a question I'm often asked. Sellers like the idea of using express mail because theoretically their letter will be opened and read immediately. I recommend express mail service when your letter relates to an important, time-sensitive offer that's highly relevant to your group, for example an event invitation.

Your offer shouldn't be a sale or discount unless it's a really significant one. That's a trick and nobody likes being fooled.

Use the informational offers mentioned in the chapter "Make an Offer They Can't Refuse." Make them time-sensitive by choosing new release offers, such as an e-book or podcast. Or express mail an invitation to a special event, such as an executive luncheon you're hosting, or a new webcast.

Follow the express mail letter with a "Did you get it?" call or email to ensure they open it and recognize its importance to them.

Sign every one. Out of the 100 holiday cards we get every year, only two have the name pre-printed on it. They're the last two we open, if we ever open them, because it's clear we don't matter enough to receive a real signature.

Show the members of your target market they matter and sign your letters—legibly. Use a blue pen so there's no doubt you signed it just for them. You want them to feel you took personal time to contact them even if they may doubt it in the back of their mind.

I sit at my home office desk on Sunday nights while watching TV and sign and stuff the letters I plan to send the next week. It doesn't take much time yet makes a huge difference in your response rate.

Hand address. Hand-addressed envelopes are opened more frequently than computer-generated or label envelopes.

If possible, write out the address. Here you can ask another person in the office to do it if you have access to someone.

If it's not possible, print the envelopes on your laser printer. When my time is limited and I'm mailing to a larger group, I choose the top 20 prospects and write their envelopes by hand.

Include your name in the return address. For all my mailings I write my first initial and last name as "K. Lee" above the pre-printed company name in the return address section. This personalizes printed envelopes, adding a projection of yourself to the outside of the letter and increasing the probability of the letter being opened.

Lumpy or flat? Lumpy envelopes with something in an odd shape inside tend to peak a prospect's curiosity and are opened more frequently than flat envelopes, although fat envelopes can be intriguing as well. Think about what you can put in your envelopes that would make them lumpy but still pertain to the message you want to convey.

Watch the message behind gimmicks. Some sellers like to use gimmicks to entice prospects to open their letters and to grab their attention immediately. One example: Sending a person a clock and enclosing a note that reads, "I am hoping you can find time to meet with me."

Although gimmicks are effective for some sellers, they may not properly reflect the image of your company or yourself. There are horror stories, too, of over-the-top or tacky gimmicks that seemed like a good idea at the time but ended up backfiring, alienating the client, or in the worst-case scenario, getting a seller fired for sending something his employer thought was in poor taste.

Carefully consider the message behind the gimmick if you choose to use one. It should fit the trigger event and your micro-segment.

Print once, mail slowly. I just told you to mail in small numbers, but who has time to print 20 letters once a week, put them in envelopes, stamp the envelop, and then mail them? Using the power of your CRM, you can set up micro-segment groups and mail in very small numbers over time.

Because there's never enough time to generate letters in small batches, I have a trick I use. I print all my letters at once with dates corresponding to the dates I'll be mailing the letters. To do this, I create the small groups I'll be mailing in our CRM and then use mail merge to create letters with different dates.

I address or print all the envelopes and as I stuff them, I write the date from the letter in the stamp area of the envelope. This is the date I need to mail the letter. When I put the stamp on the envelope, it covers my writing. Until I'm ready to mail, I can quickly sort through which envelopes need to be mailed and which ones should wait. If I hear from a prospect, I can remove that letter and not send it.

This technique allows me to print a campaign's complete set of letters or postcards at once but mail them over time and better manage follow-up.

The best days to mail. Letters received on a Tuesday, Wednesday, or Thursday have much better odds of being read than those received on a Monday or Friday. On Monday there is a greater volume of mail and email as both Saturday's and Monday's mail is delivered at the same time.

On Friday people are in a hurry to get everything done and begin their weekends. They tend to let the mail wait until Monday.

Do some tests by mailing to yourself from your office to see when the letters arrive. This helps you determine what days of the week you should mail to be sure your target market receives the letters on a Tuesday, Wednesday, or Thursday.

This test also helps you calculate when you should schedule your follow-up dates.

Don't discount your fax. Terry, one client I work with, sends letters via fax rather than the mail. People rarely use their faxes anymore and as such, he finds that his prospects are more inclined to read anything that comes through and looks important. Written on letterhead with a signature, his letters accomplish that. As an added bonus, he likes that it avoids the postage cost!

If you have access to fax numbers for your target market, you might try Terry's approach. It's especially effective in industries like financial services and healthcare where they still check their fax machines consistently.

Proof! Proof! Proof! And proof again. Read it carefully. Verify names, phone numbers, Web addresses, email addresses. If you included a product name, verify capitalization and spelling. Find the errors *before* the letter goes out!

Link to other attraction strategies. With letters and postcards, your response rate increases considerably if you combine it with other attraction strategies rather than relying on recipients to contact you.

For example, you may combine letters and emails over a six-week period, using letters to build awareness and emails as an easier response mechanism for your micro-segment. Or, you may send an invitation to an event through the mail, email several reminders to enroll, and call anybody who didn't respond. In the closing of the letter you might tell the person you will contact him by phone on a specific date and time or will send an email to set a time to meet.

In the chapter "Connect Your Efforts" I talk about linking prospect attraction activities to create campaigns. This is an effective way to increase your response rate because you are touching your target market multiple times in a short period. Many touches keep you top of mind with the prospect.

Promise follow-up. When you plan to call or stop by as your next attraction strategy, let prospects know that to create a sense of anticipation. Give a date or range of dates during which you'll be in contact.

In the body of your letter let them know how you'll be following up. Then keep the commitment and do it.

> Megan, I'll give you a call the week of August 12 to follow up.
>
> Jonathan, I'll be in Phoenix February 1st and 2nd and would be very interested in stopping by.
>
> Andrea, I'll email you a quick note next week as that may be an easier way for you to reply to me.

Some prospects look forward to your follow-up because they've already recognized they have a need. They'll plan to be available to speak with you and appreciate your extra effort.

Remember your call to action. Just because it's harder for your micro-segment to respond, don't forget the call to action. Often sellers get caught up in writing lengthy letters because they think they have more space, then forget to tell their prospects what to do.

Most successful calls to action in letters and postcards are to download something or enroll in an event. Typically prospects will not call or email you unless you've hit an immediate need they have. This is why you want to combine letters with another attraction strategy.

Consider an Awareness-only Mailing

If you aren't yet well known in your target market, you may choose to execute a series of letters or postcards at the start of your attraction campaign. Your purpose in these mailings is not to get leads, albeit that would be nice.

Although the letter inside must be well-written, there's a high probability the envelope will never be opened because the prospect hasn't heard of you or your company. In this type of mailing, your purpose is to begin creating awareness for your own and your company's name.

Prospects receive the letter and see your name. After sending three letters your name begins to register with them. They probably don't remember that you've mailed them two previous times; they just know that they've heard your name. With the fourth attempt they may read it.

You send a series of four letters or postcards, each spaced about 12–14 days apart. Each of these includes all the elements of a well-written letter in case it is opened. By the fourth attempt, they'll be aware of you and ready to pay attention.

An awareness mailing can be an effective way of getting your name in front of new prospects several times over a period of a few months. When you call or email, they've heard of your company and perhaps even heard of you, because they've seen your name cross their desk. This increases your odds of connecting with them even if they never read one of the mail pieces you sent.

When to Avoid Letters

If your message *must* be heard or is urgent, don't send a letter. You have no guarantee prospects will open it if they don't know who you are and aren't expecting it. In this situation, you are better off calling or emailing.

When you don't have access to your target market's mailing addresses and it would require too much effort or expense to acquire them before you can execute, consider another approach.

Mailing has gotten expensive. Sometimes budget is a constraint. In that case a letter may not be your best attraction strategy. If you really like using letters, consider adapting them to send via fax.

10

Postcards and Other
Variations of Letters and Emails

* * * * * * * * * * * * * * * * * * *

I'm a firm believer in enjoying what you do, even prospect attraction and lead generation. If you're having fun, you'll be more passionate. Your energy and interest will shine through and your target market will see it. People like to work with people who are fun, passionate experts.

You want your personal attraction strategies to feel fun, too. When you do, people will pay attention. They'll remember your name, or at least your company name. When you call and mention your postcard, they'll say things like, "Oh, I remember that postcard! It had a funny cartoon." Or, "Oh I remember you. Didn't you send that postcard from the beach in Florida?"

Our goal in lead generation is to get people to remember us and respond. Postcards, fun letters, and witty emails accomplish that.

There are myriad variations of letters limited only by your imagination. Link them to your attraction campaign to add some fun for yourself and your prospects. Use the content to demonstrate your expertise and passion. This chapter will get your ideas flowing.

I guarantee that your personal approach will attract new clients when they have a need.

Postcards

Postcards have become a popular alternative to letters because they don't require opening. The belief is that the probability of your message being read increases. But while it may get read, there's no guarantee it'll make it past the gatekeeper to the business owner or executive you're targeting.

Here are some ideas to move beyond the boring business postcards and increase your chances of breaking through the gatekeeper. Use the same strategies as letters for addressing, mailing, and proofing.

Create a campaign. One postcard probably won't generate many responses. It's too brief. Use them in conjunction with other attraction strategies or create a series of them to generate interest.

Include a call to action. Even though there isn't much space for a message, include a requested action. It could be to download a recent report, read an article, or save the date for an upcoming event. Keep the title of the offer short and simple. Be clear what action you want contacts to take and make the offer high quality.

Include your contact information. In case they're interested, you want them to know where to call or email to reach you.

Handwrite. If your group is small, plan to handwrite the postcard. Create the message you want to say just as you would for an email or a letter. Proof and spell check. Then write it on all the cards.

Use postcards from a recent vacation. They'll get read for sure because of the interesting picture. Begin or end with a comment about the origin of the postcard that gives a bit of insight into you.

> The snow was fabulous in Breckenridge this week! I just love the view from the peak.

> Disney World was exhausting but fun—except for Tower of Terror. That's just terrorizing!

Holiday Greetings

Many business people send holiday greetings in December. Some have caught on to sending them at Thanksgiving. Consider sending yours during unusual holidays when your micro-segment isn't expecting them.

Mail or email? Your greetings can be physical cards or electronic versions. That doesn't matter. They get opened because of the unusual timing.

Use a different call to action. Unlike the other personal attraction strategies, holiday cards do not have an overt call to action. The implied call to action is to respond wishing you a happy holiday as well.

Every time I send a holiday card, I get leads. People respond saying how nice it is to hear from me and ask a question about an offering or suggest we set a time to talk. Not all prospect attraction strategies have to be overt requests for business. Sometimes they're just checking in to remind your contacts that you're still there, thinking of them.

While social media does basically the same thing, your comments can get lost in between everyone else's. These messages are more personal, special and fun.

Holiday messages. Here are examples of several appropriate holidays to use and their key messages:

HOLIDAY	KEY MESSAGE
New Year	Wishing you a successful year; looking forward to working with you in the new year.
Valentine's Day	You are special to us.
Memorial Day	Thinking of you.
Summertime	Wishing you the opportunity to relax and enjoy the warm weather with your family and friends.
Thanksgiving	Thank you for being a client.
December Holidays	Enjoy the holiday season; looking forward to working with you in the new year.

I find holiday cards are especially successful when sent at a time when people least expect a card. I've sent cards for Thanksgiving, Valentine's Day, and the beginning of summer. They always get a strong response.

Incorporate holiday cards into your attraction campaign. Holiday cards give you the opportunity to keep your name in front of your target market without feeling that you're continually pushing them. If you've been focused on a particular segment for what feels like a long time, give it a rest for a month then send a holiday card. You may plan to follow up by phone with a message that fits the card you sent and begin your conversation.

Plan time to respond. Because holiday cards are such fun, be sure to plan time on your calendar to follow up, especially if you're emailing the cards. You'll see response rates as high as 85%. Even if all people say is "you, too!" you'll want to reply to every one so they know it came from you, not the marketing machine.

Watch international holidays. If you're doing business in Asia, Europe, or Latin America be sure to send holiday cards appropriate to the country you are focused on. Also be careful not to send cards specific to a North American holiday outside North America. They not only lose their meaning but may also hurt your potential relationship with your prospects. For example, sending a summertime card in June to Australia when its winter won't have the impact you were hoping for; likewise, an Independence Day card to the U.K. or Canada in July!

Recently Published Articles

Your company may frequently publish articles. These make great offers and excellent excuses to write or email your target market.

Send out recently published articles or others that you've read and believe relate to your segment, enclosing them with a brief note. To increase the chance it'll be read, highlight the particular sections to which you want to draw your prospect's attention and then write a brief note to your contact at the top. If you're sending it electronically, quote a particular paragraph to direct her reading.

Articles are an excellent way to get the attention of your prospects because they don't feel as if you are selling. You're thinking about them and sharing something you thought would be of value.

Sales Magnet Tools for You

Visit the Sales Magnet Tool Kit for a list of unusual holidays you can use to prospect.

11

Personal Networking

For many sellers, personal networking remains their top prospect attraction approach. They find it much easier to approach a person at an event and strike up a conversation than it is to call or email. You can chat about the small stuff, learn about the other person's job and get to know something about him before attempting to set an appointment. In short, you can make a connection.

Events, both business and social, provide one of the biggest opportunities for personal networking. They can be big affairs, like trade shows and major conferences, or small ones such as a local association meeting. So, whether you're hosting or attending an event, you want to take advantage of these occasions to establish new relationships, even if like me, you're incredibly shy.

It's here that you can meet potential new customers, partners, and resources in a more personable environment: over the coffee break, standing in the buffet lunch line, mingling at the after-hours party, sitting in a session, or even from your booth.

But events aren't the only opportunity for networking. You have to be prepared to strike up a conversation no matter where you are because your next big lead could be the person sitting next to you in the coffee shop.

As much as I prefer to sit by myself, hide behind a potted plant, or disappear behind my smart phone, I've learned that the connections I make through networking can be invaluable both professionally and personally. Mix personal networking into your lead generation activities wherever you'll have face-to-face contact with prospects and the chance to stop and get to know them.

Proof That Networking Works

It's taken me all the years that we've been in business to get comfortable with networking. As much as it makes my stomach churn with nerves, I can't deny the success it's brought me and our company.

My favorite personal networking success story is the one that 11 years ago brought us one of our longest-standing client executive relationships. It started on a family cruise that we'd been looking forward to for months.

As happens before all vacations, I worked way too many hours the week prior to our departure.

We'd been asked to assist a client in developing sessions for a large conference in Miami for its 1,000+ worldwide division employees. We created the main session presentations and group activities and supplied the Master of Ceremonies for the conference.

The meeting was being held the week we were going to be on the cruise and all the materials were due the day before our family departure. As you can imagine, there was a bit of pressure at KLA Group to get everything done and ensure the client had the final materials before I left for vacation.

As luck would have it, I ended up getting sick the last day before vacation. Because it was the project due date, I continued working with our team and we completed the client's materials. It was just a stomach virus and bad as it was, I assumed I'd be better in a day or two.

So, I got on the plane and headed to the port in Puerto Rico with my husband Bill and three sons.

Well, it wasn't a simple virus after all. Three days later I was escorted off the cruise ship to a hospital in Barbados. The ship doctor didn't have the medication or equipment to help me.

If you ever need a hospital in the Caribbean, Barbados is the place to be stranded. Their skilled doctors had me stable enough to fly home within two days. Bill found me a flight with just a stop in Miami before continuing directly to Denver.

I knew our client had this huge conference going on in Miami but after mentally calculating the dates of the meeting, I hoped and prayed there wouldn't be any people from the company on my flight.

Naturally, after being sick on a beautiful family vacation why should my luck change now?

Who should sit down next to me but a man wearing a shirt with the logo of our client! Now mind you, I hadn't been out of bed since the flight to Puerto Rico. No shower, no nicely styled hair, no make-up and rumpled clothes because my suitcase was still on the ship.

After hemming and hawing about it, I finally introduced myself to the man, asked about the conference, if he'd been there, what he did. Come to find out he was an executive in charge of worldwide training for another division of our client. One of his top managers was with him, whom he promptly introduced to me.

By the end of the flight he'd given me the names of three of his managers and asked me to connect with them. So began a relationship that has generated millions of dollars and is still in place 11 years later.

You see, networking does work, and it can occur anywhere. As a seller, you have to change your perspective and live your life expecting to meet the next great prospect or alliance partner.

Networking Tips and Tricks

If you're like me and your stomach curdles at the thought of meeting new people at events you aren't familiar with, you need some tips to make your mingling a success. Even as I've gotten more comfortable with networking, I still use these techniques to ensure I get the most out of networking opportunities and avoid hiding behind the potted plant.

Identify your target connections. Take some time to identify the types of people you want to connect with at the event. Typically these are contacts in your target market or others who work with them.

There's a reason you've chosen to attend this gathering. It may be a conference focused on your micro-segment or a meeting where you can expand your own knowledge. With this in mind, consider what groups of people will be coming. Which of them do you want to be sure to get to know?

Set meetings in advance. If you have access to the participant list before the event, determine which people you want to be sure to meet. Email them in advance to set appointments. Since these are contacts you haven't met yet, suggest meeting for coffee, one of the meals, or during the trade fair.

Choose natural points in the event where breaks will occur.

Set your agenda. Before you walk into an event know what you want to talk about with people. Plan your first three questions to use with anybody you meet. Then plan the first three questions you'll ask your target connections.

You'll be prepared to have a valuable conversation with anyone rather than talking about the weather or traffic.

I use a mental agenda to help me identify what I want to talk about. It makes me more comfortable approaching people because I have a plan. Without an agenda, you reduce your odds of networking success.

Plan your conversation in your mind before it happens. On your way to the event, use your three questions to plan how the conversation will play out. Just as you prepare for potential objections in your sales calls, consider how the discussion may flow.

With little extra effort this will provide you more questions to ask and more valuable discussion points for your conversations.

What will you give? You want to make people's time spent with you to be just as valuable as you'd like your time spent with them. Know what you'll give contacts who speak with you.

Think about the type of event you are attending. If it's a conference, what good ideas and information do you have to share that'll make it interesting for people to talk with you?

What do you want to get? Consider what you want to get out of your networking conversations.

- What are the questions you want to ask?
- What do you want to learn that'll help you sell more effectively to your micro-segment?

You might be looking for information about your target market, new partners, or qualified prospects. Knowing what you want to get out of conversations helps guide your dialogues with people.

Joining a group. One of the most difficult moments at an event is when you walk into a room full of groups. People are chatting comfortably with each other and it looks as though there's nowhere for you to go—except behind the potted plant!

You can look around for someone who isn't part of a group and head over there to start a conversation.

Or, you can also join a group.

To join in, walk over and gently touch a person on the arm. The group will automatically open up and allow you to join in.

Listen carefully to the conversation. Use active listening, such as nodding and smiling, to show you're participating. Once you have an idea what's being discussed, listen for an opportunity to add to the conversation and then join in verbally. Be careful not to interrupt.

Introducing yourself. Make it easy for people to begin a conversation with you. When you introduce yourself, add a tagline they can latch on to and ask a question.

A tagline is a brief sentence you say after you introduce yourself. The tagline I use most frequently in business situations is, "Hi, I'm Kendra Lee with KLA Group. I help companies attract new prospects."

A tagline gives just enough information for the other person to ask a question to begin the conversation. Two common questions following my tagline: "What do you mean attract prospects?" or "How do you attract prospects?"

Depending on my agenda, I tweak my tagline to match my agenda. Or I follow my tagline with a question related to my agenda.

"Hi, I'm Kendra Lee with KLA Group. We help companies attract new prospects. I'm writing a book on prospect attraction, and I was wondering what the best way is for a seller to gain access to you?"

I've made it comfortable for the person I'm speaking with by giving him or her something specific to talk about, and the conversation begins quite naturally. Think about the tagline you want to use *before you arrive* at the event.

Remembering names. One of the best ways to truly connect with someone is to remember their name and use it judiciously in the conversation.

The method I've found most successful for remembering a name is to use it right away. I look into the person's eyes, studying her face at the same time, and then say, "It's nice to meet you, Elizabeth."

Partway through the discussion I use the person's name again to cement it in my memory. If I've forgotten it already, I ask right away. Because I've just met her, I'm comfortable asking again.

"I'm sorry. Your name again is . . . ?" After Elizabeth repeats her name to me, I'll say, "Thank you, Elizabeth. I'm Kendra." Repeating my name avoids Elizabeth's being embarrassed if she's forgotten my name—which she typically has!

At the end of the discourse thank the person by name once more. "It was so nice to talk with you, Elizabeth. Thank you!"

Starting conversations. Listen for other people's taglines to begin a conversation. He may have an unusual name, mention his job, or work for a company with which you may not be familiar.

I often hear, "I've only known one other Kendra," allowing me to respond, "And where did you know her from?"

You can also use your agenda to ask initial questions to begin the dialogue.

Expanding on cliché conversation starters. Yes, there are people who talk about the weather and the traffic, but you can still turn conversations that begin with a cliché into valuable discussions.

Be prepared with a few questions to ask if you are given cliché questions. Give forethought to how you can twist those questions toward your agenda.

"The traffic was terrible, wasn't it?"

"It sure was! What other events have you recently attended that had such terrible traffic, Elizabeth?"

Fact-finding through discussions. Networking provides an excellent opportunity to learn more about your target market, its business issues and needs, its industry, and your competition. Use your questioning to interview people during your conversations.

Remember the "5 W's and How" from English? Use them here to gather more information—who, what, where, when, why, and how—related to your topic. For example:

- What did you find most interesting about that last session?

- Had you heard that before? Where? When?

- Why do you think that is such an issue today?

- How is your company addressing it?

- Who else do you know here?

Be careful not to interrogate the person with questions as if you were a television reporter uncovering the story of the century. Rather, use the questions to guide the conversation and create an interesting discussion.

Don't look for leads. Let them happen. Many times sellers approach events with the intention of finding leads. Unless it's a trade show floor or lead-sharing event, that's the wrong approach. Rather, go with the intention of establishing new relationships and expanding your knowledge of your target market.

If someone comments, "Maybe you could help us." Don't immediately jump to say, "We could definitely help."

Instead, reply with a less forceful response such as, "We should explore it."

Close for a lunch or a phone meeting next week that you can turn into a real sales call. Maintain your objective to begin a relationship, not conduct a one-call close.

If the conversation is going well and the topic lends itself, you might offer to send something you think the person would find of interest. Consider this a very soft offer that furthers your connection to each other. It might include:

- An article or blog post
- An introduction to another contact
- A checklist

Ending dialogues. It's easy to find yourself joining a group and never leaving it for the duration of an event.

When you do this you limit your networking possibilities. Break out and meet a variety of people, mingling among groups.

Listen for a natural close in a topic and excuse yourself. "It's been so nice speaking with you. I look forward to talking with you again throughout the event. I'm going to circulate and meet some other new people."

If there's a person clinging to you, bring her along or introduce her to another person. "Let's go speak with that group, Elizabeth," and head over to a new group together. Or

"Elizabeth, I'd like you to meet Jeff. We work together to assist companies such as your own."

Collect cards and follow up. Throughout the event, collect cards from people you meet and want to stay in contact with. Follow up with everyone within two days of the event. Even if it's only to say that it was a pleasure to meet them you'll cement yourself in their memory.

Send a quick email. Send an invitation to connect on LinkedIn. Follow them on Twitter. If you had a valuable dialogue, link to their blog. They'll see you following them and may choose to follow you or refer you.

It goes without saying that you should follow up on leads first.

Queue follow-up emails during long conferences. During multi-day events you'll find that you've met many people and have large numbers to follow up with. Rather than waiting until I get back to the office, I write my follow-up emails before the event has ended, then queue them in my inbox to go out the day after my return. I catch people while the conference and our discussions are still top of mind.

If possible, I set follow-up appointments with people during the event while we're still face-to-face. I've even gone so far as to call assistants of people to get meetings scheduled on their calendars. Then I can let them know the next time I see them during the event that we're all set to talk on July 10. (Of course this is only when people have asked me to contact their assistants.)

Leveraging events with those who couldn't attend. Often the events you attend are targeting your micro-segment. You can use the information you gathered during sessions as a lead generation opportunity for those people in your group who couldn't attend.

Send an email following the conference that covers some of the highlights of the sessions and offer to debrief further with them in a phone meeting. If you learned something especially relevant to your target market or picked up an interesting handout, you may be able to create an offer for them. Ask that they email you if they would like a copy. When they do, you can set a time to talk with them.

What About Electronic Networking?

You bet there's a place for electronic networking in today's selling environment. We'll get to that in the Social Networking chapter.

When Not to Use Networking

What I really want to say here is that there's never a time not to include networking as a prospect attraction strategy. Removing the double negatives, that means you should always have networking as part of your strategy. That's because it's important to connect with people, and get out in public to be seen and heard. The more contacts who know you, the more people there are who can refer you.

You may choose to limit the frequency of your networking events, but be sure you're visible to your target market so you're staying top of mind with them. I recommend attending a networking event at least every six months. Many sellers choose to do it weekly and monthly.

If your funnel is empty and you need leads quickly, be sure you're networking within your target market and not in general gatherings. Stay focused on your micro-segment and places you can find them to ensure you're mingling with people who may need your services or can refer you to contacts who do.

12

Phone Pursuit

. . . .

Many books have been written about cold calling. This chapter isn't about that. It's about using the phone combined with your prospect attraction strategies to increase your odds of connecting with qualified prospects who've already expressed some type of interest.

Use cold calling when you're looking for immediate leads and your funnel is so empty you can't wait to attract prospects. You need new opportunities right now.

If you'd like to use cold calling as part of your lead generation strategy, check out the PowerProspecting Sales Kit in the Sales Magnet Tool Kit. It's got loads of ideas on how to use the phone to uncover immediate leads.

At some point in your prospect attraction campaign you need to pick up the phone and call your prospects. Integrating phone pursuit significantly increases the number of leads you will get. People are so busy today that even if they have an interest and fully intend to call you, they don't always have the time to do it. By reaching out, you capture those busy people, who by the way, are probably the ones who need your assistance the most.

When you reach out to prospects during your campaign they'll take your calls.

They'll do so because you've spent time building a relationship with them through emails, letters, events, or personal or social networking, and they feel as if they know you. You've demonstrated your expertise and if they have the problems you've been focused on they'll want to speak with you.

They're grateful you called because it was already top of mind with them to contact you. The issues you mentioned are ones they've been grappling with and they're trying to figure out how to solve. They hadn't called because they weren't sure what to do next. Now that you've called, perhaps you can direct them? Bingo, you've moved into the sales process with a new lead.

Even if your contacts aren't facing the trigger events you cited, they'll often take your call anyway.

This group wants you to know that while they don't need assistance right now, they'd like to stay in touch! This is the gift that prospect attraction strategies give to you: people who already respect you. With that respect comes the desire to learn from you, offer referrals, stay connected, and eventually work together.

It's not uncommon to reach greater than 80% of your target market during a prospect attraction campaign when you incorporate phone pursuit. One client of ours who did so reached 100% of the contacts in her target market. She was able to set appointments with interested prospects and learn companies' future plans with those who weren't ready to commit to an appointment.

Reaching out in these circumstances is much easier than ice-cold calling! You'll hear me refer to it as warm calling because you've warmed up your prospects with other prospect attraction strategies before ever attempting to call. Everybody likes to call someone who wants to talk with them, especially when the outcome could be a new prospect who has the exact issue you can address.

Phone Pursuit Tips and Tricks

Focus on those who've expressed interest. If you're looking for immediate leads, use a pursuit strategy to follow up with anyone who clicks through on an educational offer or any part of an email signature, emails you, or calls. Something about what you wrote, said, or offered peaked their interest. You can use this to begin a conversation.

If you want to nurture your leads' interest before calling, identify a specific number or type of informational offers you want them to have requested before you call them. For example, you may choose to wait until they've clicked through on three offers from an email campaign. Or you might hold off until they've downloaded an assessment checklist that indicates they're assessing their need.

Of course, you'll always want to call those who email or call you immediately because they've reached out specifically to connect with you. This is your opportunity to have a conversation and convert it into an opportunity.

Build calling into the end of campaigns. Add phone pursuit to follow up with members of your target market who haven't responded. Include it at the end of every campaign whenever you have the time or resources to do it.

This way you'll have connected with everyone in your micro-segment either through their responses during the campaign or at the end of it. You'll begin establishing more personal relationships with a larger portion of your group. People will be more open to speaking with you because you've built strong awareness throughout the campaign.

This is easier to do if you've kept your target market list small, limiting it to 150 contacts or fewer. If your list is much larger, you'll need to engage telemarketing or appointment setting resources to do the calling.

Build it into your calendar. Often it looks great in the plan to include phone pursuit, but then the time comes to execute and suddenly you find yourself unable to fit it into your schedule.

My tip here is to build phone follow-up into your calendar. Block the time in red so you won't be inclined to schedule over it.

When you write emails or letters suggesting days or times to talk, block them on your calendar as well. You're pretty safe asking a group of 75 if they're "available next Wednesday afternoon or Thursday morning to talk" because they probably won't all be open during that time. Additionally, your initial conversation generally won't exceed 20-30 minutes, so you can schedule a large number of calls within that time period if necessary.

However, if someone replies and says, "Yes, at 10:00 Thursday" you want to be able to do it. If you've already scheduled that time for another prospect, you can easily say, "By chance could you do it at 10:30?" But you certainly don't want to have scheduled a half-day off-site client meeting at that time.

Use your grabber and results. When you call, whether the contact reached out to you, or you're following up with someone who hasn't responded to any offer, use your grabber and results to start the discussion. This is what captured their attention so begin your conversation there.

As you get started, link your initial questions to the grabber you used. Or, if you've had a brief conversation via email or voicemail, use that information to begin.

> Hi Dick,
>
> It's a pleasure to talk with you! I have some ideas for you, based on several other medical practices we've worked with recently, on leveraging the stimulus package to convert your medical records to digital. I'm glad we have this opportunity to talk. [Pause for brief chit chat]
>
> How are you handling your medical records today?
>
> What are you doing already to leverage the stimulus package?

To keep your conversation focused on their priorities, ask questions associated with your grabber. Choose questions that'll provide you insight into their specific situation. With this information in hand you can easily guide the conversation and turn it into a real opportunity. It doesn't feel like a cold-call fishing expedition. You have real information you can use to make strong recommendations based on your experience.

Should You Engage an Appointment Setter?

Just like the prospects you're attempting to gain access to, you're busy. Phone pursuit may not fit in your schedule. In these instances many of our clients ponder employing an appointment setter to do the job.

Engaging an appointment setter isn't simply a matter of bringing in an experienced telemarketer, handing him the list and pointing him to a phone. To be successful, your appointment setter will need a script and training.

Have whoever knows the target market and campaign best write the script. Then schedule time to train the appointment setter how to use the script as intended.

The training goes beyond the four questions you want them to ask. To be successful it must include:

- The objective of the call

- Who the target market is

- The issues your micro-segment is dealing with that you're focused on with the campaign

- An outline of the prospect attraction campaign and what contacts have received so far

- An idea the appointment setter can share with the contact, making this more than a telemarketing call and further catching the interest of your prospects

- Up to four questions to ask to gather further insight into the contact

- Potential objections he may encounter and how to respond

- How many attempts you want him to make and with what frequency

Provide the script in two formats.

1. A conversational script that you can use to show your caller how the conversation might sound.

2. A bulleted format that can easily be referred to during the discussion without sounding as though a script is being used.

Practice with the appointment setter to be sure you're comfortable with how the calls will be conducted and if he's a strong reflection of your company. Outline when you should be alerted with an opportunity, question, or prospect's concern.

Make sure the appointment setter is excited about the micro-segment and understands your campaign. An inspired person makes much more effective calls, not to mention many more calls per day.

After the phone pursuit. Take time to meet with the appointment setter after the calls are completed. Use this as an opportunity to identify what could have been done differently to make it even more successful. Your calling person can share ideas that will improve the response rate with the next campaign.

Tips and Tricks for Avoiding Phone Tag

In today's business world it can be difficult to meet with even those people who are very interested in speaking to you. Here are some tips and tricks for what to do when you're not getting responses to your phone pursuit.

Increase your connection rate with email. We frequently play phone tag as we try to find a time for a first meeting. After two attempts to reach you, many prospects give up. Rather than lose your chance to speak with someone who's taken the time to return your call, integrate an email follow-up strategy.

Suggest specific dates and time to talk. Calendaring is one of the most challenging activities for many business owners and executives if they don't have an assistant. Personally, it's the one part of my job I can't stand. My calendar books up weeks in advance. While I may desperately want to speak with someone, I may not have an open slot for two weeks. Your calendar is probably the same and it's what happens with your contacts.

Make scheduling an appointment with you easy. Suggest two different dates and times as options to talk by phone. Include them in the voicemail you leave and follow up with an email recounting them.

Send two calendar invitations. Go one step further and send a calendar invitation if you're an Outlook or Google calendar user. Many calendar systems interface with Outlook and Google invitations and executives can quickly check their availability to accept.

I've had prospects accept calendar invitations without ever having a phone or email conversation. Remember that we said even people who're very interested may not have had the time to reply and welcome your call? Those people will accept your calendar invitation.

Schedule an appointment through the assistant. If you're lucky, the contacts you're trying to reach have an assistant. I know you're thinking, "That's lucky?" Actually it is. When you can't gain access to an over-scheduled person, assistants can help get you an appointment.

Use your trigger event with the assistant. Let her know that you have some ideas to share and wanted to spend just 15 minutes with Tom. Ask for an appointment, advising her that it's okay to confirm with Tom.

Often I find that once you're on Tom's schedule, he'll keep the 15-minute meeting. He's seen the attraction strategies you've used and received your offers. He's familiar with you and won't mind a discussion to hear some potentially excellent recommendations.

Throw them back in the pool. After nine unanswered calls or emails, stop. Clearly the timing is not right for this prospect. The trigger events and issues you've highlighted aren't a priority right now. Instead of continuing to poke at these people, leave them in your micro-segment and catch them with the next prospect attraction campaign you implement.

When Not to Use Phone Pursuit

When your list is large and your time limited, phone pursuit may not be your best attraction strategy, even at the end of a campaign. Do use it to follow up with contacts who have reached out to you via voicemail or email, but be judicious about when you plan to use it as part of your prospect attraction campaign.

To reduce the impact on your schedule but still take advantage of the benefits of phone pursuit, divide your list and run your prospect attraction campaign in phases. Perhaps the first part of the list is run in one quarter and the next part is done in the following quarter.

Sales Magnet Tools for You

For more strategies on what to say in your initial call, get past gatekeepers and more check out the PowerProspecting Sales Kit in the Sales Magnet Tool Kit.

Part 3

Pick Your Digital Attraction Strategies

Digital

Digital attraction strategies use the internet to reach your prospects. Unlike the personal attraction strategies, you often can't control who will see your content. If you're posting articles, blogging, or using social media, anyone who is paying attention can see your content.

While at first it may appear that the lack of control is a disadvantage, it actually helps you in several ways. First, more people will have exposure to your content. If more people have exposure to your content, it opens up the possibility that they will choose to become part of one of your lists. They may subscribe to your e-newsletter or blog, connect to you on a social networking site, or register to attend an event you're hosting, to name a few. This organic growth allows you to not just expand your list, but to expand it with people who are now familiar with you and interested in learning more.

To ensure that the people who add themselves to your lists are from your target markets, you focus the content of your digital attraction strategies on trigger events they care about. Now each newsletter, blog, and social networking comment has a perspective with which people in your target market are concerned. They'll recognize it. People outside your target market typically won't be as interested and won't subscribe. In this way you're building your lists with more qualified prospects.

There are five digital attraction strategies.

1. **E-newsletters**—regular communications that keep you visible to your target market without feeling pushy

2. **Articles and blogs**—writing short editorials to demonstrate your expertise and thought leadership as both an attraction strategy and an offer

3. **Social networking**—using social networks such as LinkedIn, Facebook and Twitter to meet new contacts in your target market

4. **Social media**—using social media promotion campaigns to increase your visibility and expand your reach in your target market

5. **Online PR**—using online public relations to raise your target market's awareness of you, your company, and your offerings

Use the tips and tricks in this section to leverage the internet and digital attraction strategies to expand your reach in your target market.

13

E-Newsletters

An e-newsletter is your voice to your target market. While it's public and anyone can subscribe, your focus is on your target market. The articles highlight topics that are top-of-mind with them. All the examples relate to them. The needs you highlight are their needs. The results you talk about are the positive business changes they've experienced.

With this microscopic approach, anything you include automatically grabs their attention. Not only will they read it, but they'll watch for and share it with their peers.

Many people have avoided starting an e-newsletter because it seems like too great a commitment or too much work. However, those who subscribe to it have already begun to pre-qualify themselves as prospects. They've made the choice to follow you and what you're writing.

An e-newsletter is your opportunity to demonstrate your expertise and begin building a relationship with your prospects.

You may wonder how a relationship can possibly develop, but it does. As subscribers read your articles, see the types of events you're hosting or attending, and watch the offerings you highlight, they get to know you. You know them because they're your target market. Even though you may never have spoken directly to a particular subscriber, you know his issues because they're the same ones your other clients in his micro-segment are experiencing.

I follow the origination of our new clients to evaluate the effectiveness of our prospect attraction strategies. If a new prospect calls or emails me, I always ask how she discovered us. These strategies take time and I want to be sure we're getting a positive return when we choose to employ them. With e-newsletters, social networking, and public relations there isn't always a direct link you can attribute it to, so you have to ask.

Recently we acquired three new clients who actually picked up the phone and called us. (You know you have a hot prospect when they call you, because most frequently they prefer to send an email instead.)

When asked, all three people said, "I've been reading your e-newsletter and weekly tip for a couple of years. I wasn't sure we'd ever need your services, but have found the information quite useful. Suddenly I find we need to focus on sales and I immediately thought of you to help us."

Just like that we have a pre-qualified prospect who already knows us, understands our approach to sales, and values our expertise. After reading the e-newsletter these subscribers have confidence in our capability and feel we're the company to help them.

Interestingly, there is often no competition involved in these opportunities. The prospects called you because you're the expert they already know. They don't feel the need to shop around. I closed all three clients with a short sell cycle and we've successfully launched sustained projects across their organizations.

That's the value of an e-newsletter. They're your approach to staying in front of your target market even when you aren't running a planned prospect attraction campaign.

E-Newsletter Tips and Tricks

Keep content brief. With the advent of 140 character tweets and mobile phone access, people no longer have the patience to read long newsletter articles. I recommend that you limit newsletter articles to 350–650 words. While you'll still see articles that surpass 1,000 words, subscribers typically skim them, reading only the highlighted text and bullets unless they're very interested in the topic.

When you add information about a special offer, keep it short and include a link to learn more. Write enough that your readers know what the offer is and why they should want it. Some people will accept your offer from the newsletter. For those who need more details, send them to your website.

Make it easy to read. Most subscribers aren't willing to spend more than 5–8 minutes on your e-newsletter, and some only three minutes. They're too busy. To make sure it's a quick read:

- Include bullets and one-sentence lines. Use bold type for key phrases in the event they're skimming.

- Reduce the number of colors you use as they can be distracting or confusing.

- Watch the amount of graphics as well. If there's too much going on visually, people will simply press delete. They don't have time to figure out where to focus their attention.

Use the same format every time. As readers within your target market becomes accustomed to your publication design they'll know how they want to read it to get the maximum value from it. Choose a simple design and stick with it.

Because most languages read from left to right, place the important content to the left. Put the extras on the right. Our e-newsletter includes a box on the right side where readers can find current events, resources, and free stuff. The feature article and any special offer are always on the left.

Include just one article. While it's tempting to load down your subscribers with fabulous information you know they could use, resist temptation and include only one article per release. We know they're busy people with only 5–8 minutes available, so let's be sure not to overwhelm them and lose their attention completely.

Promote. Now that you've got your target market's attention, periodically use the opportunity to promote yourself. After the article, include information about an informational offering, event, or new resource that you want them to know about. Make it relevant to the topic of the editorial, providing the whole publication with a consistent flow. Change the promotion between releases.

Proof and spell check. No need to say more.

Include the complete content. I'm often asked if you should include the full newsletter in the body of the email, or write a brief email with lead-in paragraphs that link to the full article. After watching how prospects read emails and considering their frazzled work lives, I recommend including the full content within the body.

Consider your own subscriptions. How frequently do you skim a newsletter when it's included in the email? How often do you click through on newsletters to read an article? My guess is you graze through the ones already in front of you on your computer screen. For those requiring a click, you make a split-second decision based on the title and introductory paragraph, then delete them.

Asking your target market to click through is too much work.

Post your e-newsletter to your website or blog. Articles written for e-newsletters are ideal informational offers to use with other attraction strategies like email campaigns and events. Post both the articles and your latest e-newsletter version on your website or blog so you can reference them.

Test it on different browsers. Internet Explorer, Firefox, Safari and Google Chrome will all display your e-newsletter differently, as will mobile devices. Test it on different browsers to be sure the fonts and graphics will display appropriately if it'll be hosted on your website or blog.

Follow other people's newsletters. You'll get great ideas by watching what others do in their newsletters. Even if their topic isn't related to your own, you can see how they present content, what compels you to read it, what they choose to highlight, and more.

Attracting Subscribers

The current rule of thumb is that you need 5,000 subscribers for your newsletter be a successful business tool. While a large subscriber base does have its advantages, what's really important is that your member base consist of your target market, whatever its size. Don't worry about the size of your list. Focus instead on who's in your list.

Enticing your target market to sign up isn't as difficult as you may think. There are three essential elements to attracting subscribers:

1. Talk it up.

2. Include quality information your micro-segment cares about.

3. Make it easy to join.

Talk it up. Mention your e-newsletter in networking conversations, casual discussions, and sales calls when it fits the subject at hand.

> You should sign up for our e-newsletter. We write about current issues in information technology and offer strategies to address them.

> I'll send you a copy of the article in our latest e-newsletter. We talked about 10 email scams currently going around and how to avoid getting caught in them.

In today's world there are many other ways you can talk it up without actually talking.

- Include it in your email signature.

- Mention it in your social networking comments, referencing that you're working on an article about email scams for your upcoming e-newsletter.

- If your blog is your e-newsletter, include remarks encouraging people to subscribe to it for the latest tips on making technology work for their business.

- Send it to prospects telling them that you thought they'd find it of interest. Share it with alliance partners and vendor reps and encourage them to forward it to others who would be interested in the topic.

Remember to mention it when you have the opportunity to introduce or close an event; encourage people to sign up.

If you're speaking to a group, refer to it during your presentation. Weave it into the discussion by linking it to the topic or a question. Keep the reference to it brief. Make it just enough to wet participants' appetites so they jot it down or immediately log in from their smart phone to sign up.

> In our last e-newsletter we had an article about that exact issue. Email scams are becoming more prevalent and sneakier. We outlined 10 unique ways scammers are trying to steal something from you or just plain scare you. You have to know what you're up against and be protected.

Include quality information your micro-segment cares about. Your e-newsletter goal is to build a relationship with your subscribers so that when they have a need you can fulfill, you're the first person they call.

To accomplish this it's imperative that the article be value-packed and full of relevant information. Your micro-segment must feel that you know them and are providing details they need and want to know.

We'll go into depth on how to write compelling articles in the chapter, Articles and Blogging.

Make it easy to join. After talking up your e-newsletter, be sure that it's simple for people to enroll. Post a prominent "subscribe" option on your home page. Include it on other popular web pages such as the "resources" and "about your company" sections.

Add it to your shopping cart highlighting that it's "free" or "complimentary."

Include the option to enroll on all Web registration pages and event information request forms. (Read about both in the Online and Local Events chapter.)

Determine Your Frequency

You may be concerned about spamming your prospects with an e-newsletter so let's take a moment to discuss the right frequency to send it.

Remember that with today's spam laws, people must confirm a subscription to your publication. This means they've already said that they want to hear from you. Now you have to determine your best balance of communication.

Last year we simultaneously launched two new offerings for our micro-segment. We wanted everyone to know about them, so we "hit" our list numerous times over a six-week period. At the same time I had an article that had been nominated for Article of the Month by a respected organization and I wanted to win. We appealed to our subscribers for votes.

Our list received multiple weekly communications, and sometimes daily communications, within those six weeks. It's no surprise that we suddenly saw people unsubscribing. We hadn't provided sufficient valuable content mixed in with all the promotions.

Here are some questions to help you determine the appropriate frequency for your e-newsletter:

1. How frequently would your subscribers like to hear from you? Do a survey and ask them.

2. How often do you want to promote to your list? The more often, the more helpful features they need to receive to balance the marketing.

3. How much time do you have to write stories that your subscribers will appreciate?

4. What's the availability of your resources who'll post and send the e-newsletter after you've written it?

Some companies opt for weekly e-newsletters. Others are bi-monthly, or monthly. Choose what works best within your own resource constraints and for your target market. To maintain visibility to your subscriber target market, I recommend releasing a new issue at least once a month but no more than once a week.

Blogs are different. Know that the frequency rules for blog updates are different than e-newsletters. People expect blog updates at least two to three times a week if not every day. With blogs you can get away with more frequently communication, but these posts are different than e-newsletters that include a variety of information.

Consider Starting a Blog

Blogs allow you to communicate with your subscribers much more frequently than e-newsletters. They expect to receive your ideas, recommendations, and promotions frequently but in brief posts.

Blog posts focus on one topic at a time where newsletters may include several. They are shorter in length than newsletters, generally between 50–400 words or even fewer. If there is a video, the text may include only a few sentences to entice subscribers to listen to the video.

Nearly all the same tips for e-newsletters apply to blogs. Your objective is to gain a subscriber base of people within your target market and begin establishing an on-line relationship with them. This will keep you at the forefront of their mind when they need assistance you can provide.

Another advantage of a blog is that other blogs can link to it. If they like your content, they may mention it on their blog, or even make you a regular feature on it. This extends your visibility beyond your subscribers and drives new subscribers. As more people become exposed to your blog, they'll subscribe.

When Not to Use E-Newsletters

E-newsletters are a long-term approach to attracting prospects. While you'll extend offers in them to attend events or to sign up for a new service, most people use them for the information you provide. As they get to know you, you gain credibility with them. It's after this credible relationship is established that they begin to think of you as someone who could help them with their business issues.

When you need prospects immediately, e-newsletters aren't the most effective approach unless you've had an established subscriber base that's been following you for 18 months or longer. If you have an established membership, you can use your e-newsletter list to mine for new prospects.

14

Articles and Blogging

· · · · · · · · · · · · · · · · · · ·

Articles and blogging are an ideal way to demonstrate your expertise and they can be leveraged across all your attraction strategies. They serve as an attraction strategy on their own while serving as offers for other attraction strategies.

Your micro-segment reads your articles just like your e-newsletters and gets to know you through them. These subscribers experience your knowledge, listen to your recommendations, and try your ideas. You become the specialist they turn to on your subject.

Your articles are saved on hard discs, passed around at meetings, forwarded to teams, archived on article sites, and more. You're able to leverage them over a long period of time. An article I wrote three years ago is one of the highest-ranked articles on a website we post to. Even when you know things have changed and you might discuss the topic differently today, readers are still finding beneficial information in it.

If you're a good writer and like expressing your opinion or sharing ideas, articles and blogging will be effective techniques for you to uncover new prospects.

Many people shy away from writing articles because they appear hard to do. They don't know what to write or aren't confident in their writing style. The blank page intimidates them. Yet you have so much knowledge about your target market that you can draw from to create a respected article.

If after reading this chapter you still feel this isn't for you, dip your toe in by commenting on other people's blogs. You'll have an opportunity to see how your micro-segment responds to your posts. You'll refine your writing and perhaps even build your confidence to try an article.

If you're excited about the opportunity to share your ideas in writing, you may find that you enjoy it so much that you want to start your own blog!

Article and Blogging Tips and Tricks

Pick your topic. Choose topics that are priorities for your target market. Frame your writing around issues they're grappling with or trigger event they're experiencing. Focus on subjects they're passionate about rather than a product feature. Consider the challenges they complain about.

If you're providing recommendations, write about the definitive steps to address the topic. When you're providing facts, give examples and data. Include substantive suggestions that they can act on.

People hate it when you discuss a problem then offer only cloudy solutions. Be specific.

Give your knowledge away. The Internet has evolved to a place where companies give away free things to capture the interest of potential customers. With it, people's expectations have changed. When they read an article, they expect it to be relevant and chock full of information with details they need and want to know.

Live up to your micro-segment's expectations, then surpass them.

As the expert, provide your thought leadership for free by making profound suggestions and presenting new ideas. Openly tell them how to tackle a problem.

Direct them to places to find new answers. These may be checklists on your website, other articles, or someone else's podcast. As the master who told them how to find an answer, you're the one they'll remember.

Through your writing, give them a guidepost. Don't hold your valuable knowledge back. Use it to build credibility with your target market and start or strengthen a budding relationship.

Often sellers are concerned that if they give too much away, their customers won't need to buy anything from them. Think of this as being consultative before the sales process begins.

An article about the process to design and implement a business recovery plan can never be long enough to include all the knowledge you've amassed on the topic. Some people will be able to take the information and create a business recovery plan. But there'll be others who read the article and acknowledge that they will need help conquering the task. That's when they call you. Those prospects won't call your competitor because you're the one who wrote the detailed article, pointing out critical failure points to watch for. You demonstrated your expertise, and they want to work with the guru.

Infuse yourself. Credibility is one component of establishing a relationship with your micro-segment. The other important component is helping them get to know who you and your company are. To accomplish this, get personal in your writing.

Talk about your experiences as they relate to the subject. Offer your personal opinion. Share your own recommendations.

Start to mention a bit about yourself. This is more easily done in blogs than articles because they are more informal.

But even in an article you can infuse something about yourself. I once wrote an article about chocolate chip cookies. I love to bake and it just happened to be top of mind. I associated customer value with cookies in "Your Value is Like a Homemade Chocolate Chip Cookie." I received more emails in response to that article than I had any other. People connected with it.

Write like you talk. Add fun to your writing by using a conversational style. Talk to your reader. Use conjunctions. Get comfortable using "you" and "I."

Ask some questions. When you query your readers, you encourage them to stop and think, further engaging them with you on the topic.

Tell stories based on real client situations that'll bring your words to life for your prospect. Stories help people remember the issue as they've known it. They re-experience how it felt, and it draws them closer to you.

Avoid acronyms. Even though you're writing for your target segment, they may use different acronyms. For example, Small and Medium Business is often abbreviated SMB. However there are some companies that use SME. Spell them out first and then it's okay to use them.

Vary your words. Rather than use the same word eight times in the article, find other ways to say it to maintain interest. Thesaurus.com is my favorite resource for this task. It's always open while I'm writing.

Keep your feature brief. Here are some rules to guide your writing. Articles today tend to run between 350–650 words. Blogs tend to be between 50–400 words, however there are some writers whose blog posts are upwards of 1,000 words.

A 1,000-word composition is more like a mini-case study and must include detailed examples. For a 250-word story you can pick a topic and give a few suggestions or share a couple of concise thoughts. A 50-word post may simply share your thoughts and ask a provocative question or point you to a video.

The article average length today is somewhere between 450–500 words. That's long enough for you to discuss one problem and offer a few concrete suggestions.

Incorporate offers and calls to action. Your objective with an article is to provide new ideas that'll cause prospects within your micro-segment to take action on all the great information you've supplied. To accomplish this, invite them to take action after reading your article. Encourage them to try the ideas, think about the concepts, or change how they're doing something.

Depending on the purpose of the article or blog post, you may also choose to include an offer. You can point them to your website for a checklist or another article that goes in more depth about one area of this column.

With blogs, it's especially easy to include calls to action and offers. They simply become links within the article itself. People recognize links and instinctively click on them to see where they lead. Use this to your advantage.

Use calls to action and offers to keep your prospects engaged with you. These tools give them the opportunity to get to know you better while also educating themselves and moving them closer to wanting to work with you.

Include a brief bio in your article. Once you've written a superlative article, you want to use it as an opportunity to create awareness for yourself and your company. Move beyond saying "By Jack Thompson" under the title by including an article bio.

Your article bio is a short biography or reference about you and/or your company. It comes at the end of your article. It's the place where you can include some brief information about yourself and your company along with a link to your website or an offer to subscribe to your newsletter. In public relations lingo you may also hear it referred to as a boilerplate or byline.

Make the information you include relevant to your target market. Use this as your opportunity to continue demonstrating your expertise by reinforcing the importance of your micro-segment to your company.

My article bio reinforces my prospect attraction and small-medium business expertise while simultaneously emphasizing our company focus on small and medium size companies. You can do the same, varying your article bio if you're writing content focused on different segments.

Watch what authors include in their article bios for ideas to enhance your own.

Copyright and protect your article. Before you publish your article add the copyright notice to let people know that this is your intellectual property. This also adds credibility for you as the expert who wrote it.

Unfortunately a copyright won't stop people from plagiarizing you if they really want to steal it. For this you need to be diligent about searching the Internet to periodically identify any violators. There are a number of resources you can use to do this. One I recommend is www.copyscape.com which will search for copies of specific web pages, such as article or blog posts that others have plagiarized.

You can also do a simple internet search using a large segment of your article, such as a paragraph or several sentences. Paste a portion of your article into internet search box and press enter. If someone is plagiarizing you, the search engine will find it. You'll be able to click through quickly to find the culprit.

When you do find someone who is plagiarizing your content, take action. You can request to have your article removed from their site, or you may choose to have an attribution to you added. You'll know what your preference is based on the type of site that's using it and who it is they are targeting with their content. If necessary, get your attorney involved.

Tips for Blogging on Other People's Blogs

Regularly follow at least three blogs that your target market's involved with. In addition to writing articles, you may choose to comment on blogs your micro-segment is following. These may include industry experts, leaders, or vendors within your target market. Consistently read them and comment to be seen.

What to say. Comment from the perspective you know: Your micro-segment and the issues they're encountering. If you're an information technology professional commenting on a healthcare blog, make comments related to how technology helps address a specific topic. Or if you watched a client address a particularly difficult issue you might share some details about it even if it doesn't relate to your solutions.

Avoid brazen promotion. Your goal is to be seen as an expert for what you do, not to sell something as a result of your post. While it's tempting to try to send people to your website or get them to call you, pull back. Rather, limit yourself to mention of a resource you're aware of that may be beneficial. In today's business world it's perfectly okay to refer people to others but not acceptable to point them to yourself.

Confine your advertising to inclusion of your name, company name, and possibly website on the comment.

Use your social networking for the brazen marketing. You can always use it to point people back to a blog post through a tweet or comment as you'll discover in the next chapter, Social Networking.

Disagree professionally. When you disagree with a blog post, don't disparage it. Be professional and support your opinion. Remember that electronic media is stored in many places and once a comment is posted, it probably can't be retracted.

Mention the blog to your target market. When you've discovered a blog that provides valuable information to your micro-segment, mention it in a newsletter, social media comment, or article. The group members will appreciate that you've alerted them to it, and the owner of the blog will be grateful for the referral. You may be asked for an interview or to contribute to the blog.

Consider a Ghost Writer or Your Vendors

If you aren't a great writer or don't have the time to do it, consider engaging a ghost writer. For years our public relations consultant wrote articles for me. I chose the topic, he interviewed me, and then drafted the article. I reviewed it and made final tweaks, adding my personal touch. It was very affordable, reduced my writing time significantly, and allowed us to consistently release new articles.

Another article source may be your vendors. Check to see if they have articles, white papers, or case studies you can leverage instead of crafting your own. As you choose which ones to incorporate into your prospect attraction campaign, eliminate those that are too product-centric. For your lead generation purposes you want articles that focus on the business issues and trigger events members of your target market are encountering. It's premature to tell them what products they need to solve a problem you aren't sure they have.

When Not to Use Articles and Blogging

If you've read this chapter and the thought of writing an article or commenting on other people's blogs seems too difficult or more than you can do now, don't do it. Consider a ghost writer if you like the benefits of articles but don't want the work associated with them. This may be your fastest approach to building a library and it can be quite affordable.

Sales Magnet Tools for You

The best way to learn to write articles is to read other people's writing and determine the style you like. Check out the Sales Magnet Tool Kit for a list of websites where you can post articles for free.

15

Leverage Articles and Other People's Blogs

Once you've created an article you can use it as an offer for other attraction strategies if you just know how to leverage it. It can become an awareness-building tool extending beyond your target market. It can also serve as an offer for the micro-segment you had in mind when you wrote it.

Because an article takes time to write, consider all the ways you can employ it as a lead generation tool and do it. Don't worry that your intended prospects may see it in multiple places. They probably won't recognize it.

Recently an article of mine was promoted on several websites as well as our own. I'd sent it out in our newsletter, then learned that these other sites wanted to highlight it two months later. A number of prospects within my target market read it in our newsletter and again on one of the other websites. I knew they'd read it in the newsletter because they'd emailed me at the time to say what a great article it was. Well, I received emails again, after they'd read them on the other sites. The way the emails were written, it was clear that these people didn't even remember reading the article the first time.

Some marketers believe that a person needs to read an article or hear a concept seven times before remembering it. With this in mind, don't fret if your members of your target market may encounter your writing elsewhere. Even if they do remember it, they'll think of you as ubiquitous—everywhere they look.

Where to post your articles. To be ubiquitous and build awareness with your micro-segment, you want to post your articles to a number of different websites. This way your prospects will see your name in multiple places, keeping you in front of them and top of mind.

Many article sites allow you to simply post your article. If you meet some basic guidelines, such as no links within the body of the email and no self-promotion, your article will be accepted. These are an excellent place to begin.

There are numerous such websites for you to consider in addition to websites and blogs within your micro-segment. Start a database or spreadsheet of places to post. Each time you write a new article, post it to the sites you've identified in addition to your website.

In the Sales Magnet Tool Kit I've included links to a number of article sites you might consider.

Network with publications and bloggers your micro-segment follow. Ask clients who are members of your group what websites and blogs they subscribe to or regularly watch. Research those sites to see if they take contributed articles or if they're places you can post blog comments.

These publications are typically choosier about what they accept than article websites. They're looking for experts, ideally well-known and previously published specialists.

Even if you aren't yet widely recognized in your target market, you can still get published on these sites with a little networking.

Once you know the top sites your group follows, start a relationship with the site editors and blog owners. Call them and discuss their vision. Let them know what you're doing with their target audience in your own business. Share some client names with them to demonstrate your credibility and reinforce your expertise. Tell them where you've commented on blogs and where some of your articles are posted.

Learn what types of articles their readers like and where the publications have gaps in their content that you might be able to fill. Offer to send one or two sample stories for their consideration. Don't send more than two because the editors won't have time to read them. If you send too many articles, they'll sit unread in the inbox and you'll lose your opportunity.

Learn the editors' and bloggers' guidelines for their sites, then submit appropriate articles as you write them. It may take several months, or even a year, before they publish an article. But stick with it, nurturing the relationship. Eventually there'll be an opening you can fill.

Once they've published one of your articles, they'll likely publish more if you continue to stay in touch with them.

Use articles as offers in email campaigns, letters, and events. Every prospect attraction strategy has to have an offer to be effective. You want to entice your micro-segment to respond to you based on the business issue you're focused on and the offer you've made. Articles make ideal offers.

Use them in email campaigns, letters, warm calls, and speaking engagements. Offer them in social networking comments, and even in other articles.

As you build a repository of them you'll find that you have a wide choice to incorporate into your prospect attraction campaigns.

Comment about them on your social network. While you're creating, comment about it on your social networks. Mention the topic and what you're writing it for. Include a few sentences about the topic. When it's done, talk about that, too. Include the final article title with a link to where your followers can read it.

After you've made a particularly enlightening comment on someone else's blog, comment about it on your own social networks and include a link for others to read what you wrote. You may also choose to repeat a portion of the comment as well.

Share them with your alliance partners. Your alliance partners are looking for content to include in their newsletters and prospect attraction strategies just as you are. Share your articles with partners and encourage them to use your writings with their clients and campaigns. Include your article bio and copyright just as you would for the article websites and don't be concerned about your intellectual property.

As they incorporate your articles into their strategies it extends awareness for you and your company into new target markets. You'll find that you gain new subscribers and followers through their efforts.

Search Engine Impact of Duplicate Postings

Your objective in lead generation is to reach your target market wherever they may be to get more prospects and fill your pipeline. This means that you want to be seen wherever your prospects might look so you can grab their attention. Posting articles on various sites they frequent helps you accomplish this objective.

However, if you also have a goal for your website or blog to rank highly through search engine optimization, you may not want to post articles in multiple sites. Search engines now penalize content that can be found on multiple websites on the internet. This means that if you post an article on two or more websites, it won't rank as high as an article that's only available on one website.

If one of your lead generation strategies is to use search engine optimization to attract prospects, consider posting only a few of your articles on multiple sites. For highly relevant and timely content, ensure it's only available on your website. This will help you maintain your ranking, while still making your content available in other places your prospects may be looking.

If you don't feel comfortable with even limited duplicate posting, consider writing original articles for use only on the additional sites you've identified. This will require more writing on your part, but it will avoid the risk of any impact on your search engine ranking, while still keeping you visible to your prospects from multiple websites.

When Not to Leverage Articles and Blogs

Like e-newsletters, articles and blogs are a long-term approach to attracting prospects. If you need prospects right away, only write articles or blog posts that can be used immediately as informational offers in your prospect attraction strategies. Wait until the pipeline is full to begin creating a library of articles.

16

Social Networking

* * * * * * * * * * * * * * * * * * *

Social networking has become the rage both professionally and personally. There's much I could write about how to use it, but the focus of this book is on prospect attraction and getting prospects to contact you when they have a need. With that in mind, let's stick to how we can use social media to get new qualified contacts to follow, watch, and respond to you. That means we want to use it to gain awareness and generate interest from our target market.

There are a variety of social networking options and the number keeps growing each week as more are added. For prospect attraction purposes, you want to be present on the ones that your target market is following. Today, the most popular are Twitter, Facebook, and LinkedIn. Depending on who your top micro-segments are, you may also need to be seen on others that aren't as well-known.

The easiest way to determine which networks to get involved in is to ask current clients in your target markets which networks they engage in today. However, you may discover that you have some customers who are active and others who discount the value of social networking.

The challenge in setting up your social media prospect attraction strategy is that members of most industry verticals aren't participating in any one particular network. By their very nature, social networks cross regions, countries, and hemispheres. Similarly, they extend across age groups from teens to seniors.

There isn't any true segmentation in these mediums. Choosing to be active in just one won't put your in front of all your target prospects. You have to be active in the top networks being used by members of your micro-segment.

If you like the idea of using social networks to attract prospects, I recommend you choose three social networks and get started.

Why Bother?

If you're like me, you'll enter into social networking kicking and screaming. I was already a power LinkedIn user but hadn't committed to Facebook or Twitter. They didn't feel professional enough to me and I couldn't see how I could possibly add another thing to my already too-busy days. But since the Information Technology industry is one of our target markets, you can imagine that great groups of our qualified prospects already were getting involved.

I didn't have a choice.

Once I dipped my toe in, I discovered it was actually fun! It wasn't a hardship to stay current on Facebook and Twitter. In fact, I had to make a conscious effort not to spend too much time on either.

What I learned is that the people who engage in social networking pay attention to different attraction strategies.

They respond to LinkedIn InMails or Twitter direct messages. They click through to articles mentioned in Twitter tweets and sign up for events posted in Facebook or LinkedIn, but may not respond to an email campaign or a personal letter.

All of the sudden I was reaching a broader number of my micro-segment in ways they found easy to respond to. I was attracting an incremental number of prospects using LinkedIn, Twitter, and Facebook.

They were contacting me using those same media, asking for additional information and appointments all because I'd expanded my attraction strategy to include social networking! You can have the same success.

Social Networking Tips and Tricks

Create an attention-getting profile. Set up your profile to highlight your expertise and help viewers get to know you.

Insert a picture but choose one that fits the style of the social network. In Facebook, make it personal; LinkedIn, professional; Twitter, either, depending on how you're using it. Allow people to see your smiling, friendly face!

Include one or two personal interests, giving people something that'll help them relate to you as an individual. List schools you went to and associations you're involved with; anything that'll help you create a connection.

In LinkedIn, be sure you have several current recommendations written by members of your micro-segment. These provide instant credibility and elevate your level of expertise. Anyone who views the profile of the person who recommended you also sees the recommendation and can view your profile.

Allow public access to your profile and enter contact information to make it easy for people to find and follow you.

Put a public link to one or two of your social network profiles in your email signature. You'd be surprised how many people click through to read it and follow you.

Get the right followers. The trick in successful prospect attraction through social media is to get your target market to follow you. To do that, you start by following them or inviting them to follow you. In social networking, when you extend an invitation, most people accept it.

Only a few scrutinize invitations to determine if they want to accept or not, especially on networks like LinkedIn. On Facebook some people are more careful only to accept requests from friends. On Twitter you can follow anybody you want. If they don't want you following them, they actually have to go in and remove you from their followers list.

Start by following people in your micro-segment. Then look for industry leaders or other leaders in the segment and get connected to them. Join lists and groups your target market frequents. Be everywhere they are.

Don't worry about how many followers you have. Focus on securing connections from your primary segment.

Broaden your connections. Don't be so choosy about who you allow to connect to you in LinkedIn and Facebook. You're in sales. You try to network with as many people as you can at face-to-face events. Now extend that philosophy to your online social networks, too. Let your micro-segment and experts within it get close to you. Accept their invitations and make it known in your profiles that you welcome invitations.

Get to know your target market. Social media is an excellent tool for learning about your group. Research their profiles and comments to gain insights into who they are, their level of experience, and what they're thinking about. Use this information to:

- Pinpoint trigger events or business needs to focus on
- Determine article or blog topics that'll grab their attention
- Recognize the types of events that'll interest them
- Make relevant comments they'll watch
- Select intriguing offers

Establish your expertise. Your followers are watching you, the individual. They aren't interested in your products. This is your opportunity to establish yourself as the expert so concentrate on building your image.

Make your comments relevant to your target market. Yes, you'll have followers who aren't in your micro-segment, but your statements aren't for them. Frame your thoughts around topics that interest your target market and items they need to hear or know.

Mention who you're working with. Another way to establish your expertise is to comment about people you're talking with and the type of work you're doing. This is especially true when you're working with a thought leader or someone who's highly respected by members of your target group. Similarly, if you're helping a client address an issue you know many in your micro-segment are grappling with, remark about it.

Be casual and relaxed. Social networking is so popular is because it allows people to be themselves, talking about what's top of mind with them. To fit in and to be followed it's important that your comments are casual, relaxed, and a reflection of yourself.

Not every statement needs to be insightful and quotable. Provide your connections insight into you as a person. This is especially important on Facebook, which is a much more personal network than LinkedIn and Twitter.

Mention when you're working on a hobby or doing something fun. Let your followers get to know you, start to like you, and want to work with you.

Join groups and get involved. If your social network has groups, join the ones your target market follows. Get involved by participating in and starting discussions. Post articles and ask questions related to the topic. Post events and invite members to sign up and attend.

Create groups and lists to manage contacts. Some social networks allow you to create groups and lists to manage your contacts.

On Facebook and Google+, you can use groups to segment your connections. This allows you to comment only to that group, keeping your posts pertinent and interesting.

On Twitter, you can use lists to manage who you're following and quickly review and respond to comments of people in the group. For example, you may set up lists for customers, prospects, marketing gurus, and industry experts. Now if you want to retweet an industry expert, you don't need to scroll through all your tweets to find one. You can see the comments of the people in your list and easily retweet one or several with little time invested.

Include short, trackable links. The value in social media is in being heard. But often you aren't sure if anyone is listening. Use trackable links and analytics to identify what types of offers your followers are responding to, the days and times they're listening, the topics they like and more.

If using analytics seems a bit too complex for you, simply use trackable links such as www.bit.ly. With a quick refresh of your screen you can see how many people clicked on a particular link, on what date, and at what time. You'll instantly know if what you commented about caught their attention.

To use it, take the link you want to insert in your comment and convert it to a shorter link. There are a number of tools available to shorten links, such at www.bit.ly, www. tinyurl.com or www.short.lk. Choose one that'll allow you to analyze click-throughs.

Be consistent. As with blogging, once you begin using social networks and attracting followers, you have to maintain them consistently. This means you need to comment, not just with a consistent message but also in a timely, regular manner.

Many people are concerned that they need to spend hours a day on social media. This isn't the case at all. Set aside specific times to do it: Thirty minutes a day to focus on reading what your network is writing and on making your own comments. If that's too much, spend 30 minutes every other day. The point is to get started.

Once your followers start paying attention, you want to stay visible to them.

Stay professional. It's widely known now that Human Resources departments review social media sites before hiring and firing people. Your prospects and potential partners can do the same. Never post or say anything that you wouldn't want the whole world to know.

Some key areas to avoid:

- Incriminating pictures
- Comments made in the heat of the moment

- Private information about your family, clients, prospects, and alliance partners
- Private information about your company and offerings

All social network information is stored somewhere. While you may delete it, someone has backed it up. Keep your comments and information professional to avoid future issues.

Social Networking for the Advanced

As you've probably noticed by now, each social network has its own unique personality.

For example, LinkedIn is professionally focused. Comments, news, events, and groups are all centered on business topics.

Facebook is personal. Users talk about what's happening in their lives. There are business fan pages, and while people do mention what they're doing at work, their comments are much more personal than professional.

Twitter is a combination of professional and personal. The mix depends on who you're following. For prospect attraction purposes, your mix of comments depends on who your target market is and what they want from you. If you're an entertainer attracting new viewers, your tweets will be more personal to let people feel like they have access to you the star. If you're a software provider, your tweets will probably be more heavily weighted toward the professional so you can establish your expertise.

What this all means to you if you want to take your social networking to the advanced level is that you need to tailor your comments to the personality of the network.

There are many tools that allow you to post comments across multiple networks, such as Hootsuite and Tweetdeck. They're very efficient but when you're trying to get personal with your primary group, you don't want to be merely efficient. You also must be effective.

As you use these tools, consider how you can make your comments feel personal to your target market. Choose carefully which comments you're going to publish to all networks at once and which statements it makes sense to edit slightly to fit the personality of the social network.

- Your Facebook friends and LinkedIn connections don't appreciate seeing a "#Prospecting" or "RT @JacksonSmith" in their comments meant for a Twitter network.

- A 140-character Twitter comment or LinkedIn status update sticks out blatantly in Facebook. Unless you're a gifted writer, it's often too short and dry for Facebook's friendliness.

When I see these types of comments inappropriately posted on a social network it feels as if someone just cold-called their social connections with a generic message. The comments don't feel personal to the micro-segment in any way. Over time your connections lose interest and stop reading what you're writing. You lose the effectiveness of your prospect attraction efforts.

Always be aware that your social networking objective is to get closer to your target market, demonstrating your expertise by providing valuable comments and information. Then, when qualified prospects have a need, you'll be top of mind and they'll reach out to you.

When Not to Use Social Networking

Social networking establishes you as an expert and gives your target market insight into you personally. It's more about you than your offerings. While some people use it to promote product specials it's more effective in promoting your prospect attraction strategies such as events, blogs, articles and press releases.

One of the greatest values of social networking is that your followers are able to get to know you without engaging if they so choose. They don't need to sign up for an event to hear your ideas. They don't need to fill out a form on the website to read an article. They can quietly watch and learn about you. As they experience your expertise over time, they also become comfortable with you and your capabilities. They'll approach you when they finally have a need.

If you're looking for immediate leads, social networking won't be the most efficient strategy. It takes time for your target market to notice and then follow you. It is very effective when followers finally do notice you and need your assistance.

Social networking will help drive traffic in your other prospect attraction strategies where you do get immediate leads.

Therefore, if you're new to social networking, or haven't built a following from your micro-segment, start getting active, but don't expect immediate leads. Do integrate social networking with your other prospect attraction strategies to boost exposure and broaden your reach to new contacts.

Getting Started

The best way to get started with social networking is to just do it. Sign up for Twitter, Facebook, and LinkedIn. Set up your profile and start getting involved.

Connect with and start following people you respect. Watch what they're commenting about and posting. You'll quickly find your own style.

You can connect to me on any of these social networks directly from the Sales Magnet Tool Kit main page.

17

Use Social Media to Promote Other Attraction Strategies

• • • • • • • • • • • • • • • • • • •

One advantage of social media is that you can use it to drive traffic to your other prospect attraction strategies such as blogs, events, articles, newsletters, and press releases. With social media you're able to broaden visibility into what you're doing across your target market and attract even more new contacts.

You can double the number of people who attend an on-line event you're hosting. You can triple or quadruple the number of people who read a new article you've written. When your followers share comments you've made about a new article, press release or event, suddenly the sky is the limit for the number of people who may see it and take action.

For this reason I integrate social media into every lead generation activity we do. And every time, we see results through increases in our lists, participation, and leads. I challenge you to use these techniques to leverage your efforts in your prospect attraction strategies and increase your own response rates.

Do some electronic networking. When people send you an invitation, thank them via the internal email system, then do a bit of quick research in their profile. If they're a potentially qualified prospect in your target market, suggest a meeting based on the trigger events and business issues you suspect they have.

Promote links. Whenever you've written a new article or published a press release, write about it and include a trackable link. When you've just read a good blog and posted a response, mention it and include a link. Get creative and whenever possible include a link that'll provide more information and expand your micro-segment's knowledge in valuable ways.

Mention new offers in the making. While you're writing articles, ebooks, and blogs or designing an upcoming event, comment about it. Use titles and key words so search engines pick up on them. They'll also begin to build awareness around the topic.

Post articles. While you want to post articles on your website, leverage your social networks to post them where active members can see them as well.

In LinkedIn, post them in the News section of groups. Comment about them in your status. Be sure to click the box to request notification when someone comments so you can see their comment and reply back.

On Facebook, post articles on your fan page if you have one. On Facebook and Twitter, comment about them and include a link.

Comment after posting to a group. After starting a discussion or posting an article, make a comment. People scanning new postings will notice the comment following yours and stop to read it. Your article will get more visibility.

Leverage your network. Ask your network of top clients and peers to comment and tweet about a blog entry, article, event, or press release. Give them brief phrases they can simply copy and paste.

Have them note on LinkedIn and Facebook that they're interested in attending an event you're hosting. Your message will reach out into their contact base, further extending your reach even though they aren't attending.

Send prospecting emails. Once you have a group of followers from your micro-segment, you have another list you can send to. You're no longer limited by your list of people for whom you have email address. Extend your prospecting email campaign for use in LinkedIn and Facebook where you can send direct messages.

In LinkedIn you can send a direct message to anyone you're connected to, as well as anyone who's in the same group. The benefit to you in doing this is that typically LinkedIn direct messages will make it past spam filters into your prospect's inbox. Not only can you be certain it was received, but often people read their LinkedIn direct messages more carefully.

As a word of caution, if you're going to use LinkedIn or Facebook to send direct prospecting emails, be certain they are of high value, focusing on a trigger event or business issue. If they're an obvious solicitation, you'll receive a scathing email in return, be blocked from future communications, and quite possibly be reported for improper use.

Special Tips and Tricks for Events

With today's technology, events are inexpensive to run. But if you're going to do all the work to create great content with high value, you want to be sure that the people who are interested in it know it's happening and how to sign up.

You won't get the number of qualified leads you deserve if only five people attend! Here's where social media can help.

Post the event details on your website. This is your opportunity to say as much as you'd like about the event, including every fact. Point all your comments back to your website for additional information and registration. Not only do interested readers learn more about the event, now they're on your website, too.

Post everywhere. Lots of people don't realize that you can post events to LinkedIn and Facebook in special "Event" sections. Once you do, people connected to you are notified, and others outside your group see them when they use keyword searches. Your network can forward the link on to others in their groups who might be interested, too.

Talk up events. Comment about an upcoming event in your LinkedIn status. Discuss it on Facebook. Tweet about it. Carry your statements over the course of days and weeks preceding the event, right up to minutes before it begins. Always include a registration link.

Attract interest through enrollees. As people from your target segments enroll in an event, shoot them a quick email and ask them to click in LinkedIn and Facebook that they're attending. Send them the direct event link to make it simple for them. Now all their connections see that they're attending, expanding your message within your target market to new contacts.

Get new prospects after the event. After the event, write about how it went, the questions that were asked, the type of people who attended. Include a link to an offer related to the event, perhaps a recording of it, a copy of the slides, or an article about the topic.

Once your content is perfected, events are a numbers game. The more interested people from your target market you can attract to your event, the greater the number of leads.

Social networking can get your message out, bringing participants and leads to you!

When Not to Use Social Media to Promote Other Attraction Strategies

Be careful not to promote client information in your social networking unless you want others to know about it. Everyone from the client himself to your competition may see it. Sometimes this is part of your strategy and your clients appreciate the additional exposure. Just be sure this is your intention before you make the comments.

If you're in a highly competitive market and your social promotion will reach competitors you don't want to learn about your new direction, offerings or events, limit your promotion to prospect attraction strategies that allow you to better control who receives and reads it. In this situation, don't avoid social networking. Instead, keep your commenting more broad and general.

18

Online PR

· ·

The purpose of public relations is to raise your target market's awareness of you, your company, and your offerings. On its own it won't attract prospects as effectively as an email campaign or event, however it will keep your name in front of your micro-segment, just as social media does. A qualified prospect with a need will call you because of the exposure you've generated for yourself.

In this way, public relations can have a tremendous impact on your business through the credibility and visibility it provides. If you write articles and put them on the Internet you're going to drive traffic to your site. If you get quoted in the national or local media, people will see your name and want to do business with you.

There are two types of public relations you can do: online and off-line. In this chapter we'll look at all the things you can do to promote yourself online. Later we'll look at more traditional, off-line PR activities as part of the collaborative attraction strategies.

Online PR is different than social media in that public relations activities are your opportunity to shout about your outstanding achievements. This attraction strategy is all about you and how you've helped your customers overcome their business issues.

Typically people think first of press releases when they think of online PR, however it can also include:

- Podcasts, YouTube Videos and other recordings
- Case studies and white papers
- Testimonials
- Interviews
- Articles
- Ebooks
- Tools like worksheets, self-assessments and checklists
- Social commenting

These are all activities that get your name out in front of your micro-segment. Notice that each of these examples can also be educational or informational offers for other attraction strategies, such as letters, events, email campaigns, and social networking.

This means that you get double use from them when you employ online PR: as an attraction strategy on its own, and as an offer within another attraction strategy. For this reason I use a lot of online PR as part of our attraction strategy campaigns at KLA Group. It reduces the amount of effort we have to exert simultaneous to increasing our exposure and repository of offers.

Here are my top suggestions for online PR.

Write Articles

This is one of the best ways to get publicity on the internet. Craft informational articles that teach your target market how to do something. For example, "The Top 10 Ways to Build Rapport", or "Twelve Steps to a Secure Computer System."

Keep your story related to what you sell, but focused on issues your prospects are facing. Write as if you're writing directly to them.

At the end of the article include a subtle call to action to attract prospects. For example, "To learn 25 more tips to securing your data, visit our website."

Post your articles on internet sites that your micro-segment frequents.

If you can draft a to-do list, you can craft an article. For more on writing and posting articles, see the chapters *Articles and Blogging* and *Leverage Articles and Other People's Blogs*.

Be available for interviews.

You may have already decided that articles aren't your thing and that's okay. Journalists are always on the lookout for good resources. If you've been able to impress the media with your expertise, make yourself available for interviews and let them write the articles.

It's easier than ever to meet journalists. Connect with them on your social networks and start conversations about articles they've written or comments they've made.

Start a relationship with those who work with your target market. Share your experiences and observations. Introduce them to clients of yours that would make good subjects for stories. Often they'll ask to quote you in the same story.

Subscribe to www.helpareporter.com. It's a site that publishes a list of reporters looking for people to interview for stories they're working on. The list comes out three times a day. Skim it for features that look relevant to your segment, then contact the reporter directly.

As reporters get acquainted with you, they'll reach out to you for quotes and introductions. They may even ask you to comment on a blog they're writing or a podcast they're recording. Always make yourself available for interviews based on the reporter's schedule. They're under tight deadlines and can't wait until your schedule frees up.

Involve clients. If your customers are doing something that's newsworthy, ask them if you can present their story to one of your media contacts. The publicity will help gain your clients exposure they'll be grateful for. It'll also provide your journalist contacts with another good story angle. It'll be a win for your clients, the press, and you.

Write the interview yourself. Many blog owners use written interviews with experts to drive subscribers and traffic. Their subscribers enjoy reading conversations that provide multiple perspectives. Frequently these interviews are actually written by the expert, not the blog owner.

To have an interview with you posted on the blog of a thought leader in your target market, send a pre-written interview on a topic you think his subscribers would find of interest. Write both the questions and your answers. Format it similarly to other interviews you've seen on the blog.

Now you've made it simple for the owner to use when he's at a roadblock and low on content.

After it's posted, be sure to comment about it and link to it from your own website. Respond to comments readers' make. Incorporate it as an educational offer in another of your prospect attraction strategies. The fact that it's on another person's blog only increases the respect your micro-segment readers will have for you.

Record Podcasts

You might wonder why you'd record a podcast instead of a video. With the popularity of the iPod, audio appeals to people who want to listen and learn. For you, the technology is easy to use and often less expensive than video.

You no longer need expensive recording equipment.

You can record a podcast directly to your PC using a tool like Audacity. Or, you can record it on a telephone conference line like www.freeconferencecall.com or www.instanttele seminar.com. If you'd like a professional recording with lead-in and follow-up music, editing and polishing you may choose to engage a service like www.GreatTeleseminars.com.

With any of these formats you can have a podcast ready for posting in an hour or less.

Make it worth their time. Many podcasts are typically only 3–5 minutes in length, although they can go as long as 50 minutes using a format more similar to a webcast.

Use brief podcasts to delve into one key point, giving valuable information and offering how-to recommendations. Provide just enough information to wet your target market's appetite to learn more on a related topic.

Short podcasts are an excellent offer to accompany an email or letter because they're so quick to listen to, provide immediate suggestions, and instantly demonstrate your credibility.

Longer podcasts are ideal offers for educating prospects in your target market. Choose a topic that's new to them but of high interest, such as how to draft a business interruption plan or how to leverage the economic stimulus package to upgrade their IT infrastructure. Provide some background on the situation and why they should care about it. Incorporate resources and as with shorter podcasts be certain to include valuable recommendations to address the issue.

At the end of all podcasts include a call to action to do something, such as listen to another podcast, read an article, take a survey, or contact you.

Make it a case study. Consider creating an audio case study. Highlight the issues a client was grappling with, how he came to a decision to address them, and what solution you recommended and implemented. Conclude with the business results the client experienced after the issue was handled, including both quantitative and qualitative information.

Distribute. Post your podcasts on your website or blog. Make CDs to leave with clients and prospects on sales calls. Refer to them in other prospect attraction strategies.

Search the Internet using the phrase "how can I distribute my podcast for free" for the latest places to post.

Get recorded by others. If you aren't keen on creating your own podcast, many people look for expert guests to interview for their podcasts. Find the experts in your target market who do this and make yourself available for their shows. Offer to promote the podcast to your subscriber list and target market in exchange for sharing your expertise in an interview.

Record Videos

Video cameras and microphones have come down in price significantly in the last few years with the computer software available to support it. You may even have this capability built into your smart phone. Not many sellers in the business world are incorporating video into their prospect attraction, making it a huge opportunity if you're comfortable with it.

The fact that those in your micro-segment can see and hear you makes them even more comfortable with you.

Use the same approach as with podcasts, keeping your content of high informational value. Incorporate yourself, graphics, and music to make it even more interesting.

Post your videos to YouTube, a standard anybody can link to and view. Include them on your website or blog, too, then promote them as offers in your prospect attraction strategies.

Create a Wall of Fame

The real reason you're doing publicity is to create visibility and credibility. Once articles are printed, you've been quoted, or a podcast has been posted, you have credibility. Now it's time to leverage it.

Create a Wall of Fame on your website and in your office listing all the places you've been quoted and published. Link to every site and list the articles or quotes. Maintain it, consistently adding new sites as your visibility expands.

Publish Press Releases Online

The latest trend for press releases is to publish them to the Web first and traditional print publications second. The decision-makers in your micro-segment are likely business owners and executives who find their information on the Internet. They probably subscribe to RSS feeds, read blogs, and research via the web.

With this in mind, you want your press releases published in places your target market will encounter them and read about what's happening in your business. This can be done via a local PR firm or a web based PR service.

Local PR firms can be pricey, but bring the added benefit that they get to know your company intimately. They maintain a database of media contacts and relationships. The local firm will write your press releases, then submit them to their contacts. In addition to assisting with press releases, they're able to make publicity strategy recommendations as well as secure interviews and article spots in print publications.

Web-based PR services typically maintain a database of hundreds to thousands of media contacts that you can tap into. For example, at last check one Web service had contact information for 482 journalists in print media, radio, and television in the Omaha, Nebraska area alone.

With Web-based PR services, you sign up, post your press release, and let them promote it to the groups of journalists you identify. Many of these services have tutorials on how to write a press release including examples and templates so you don't have to figure it out on your own.

Write two releases. We write two releases when we create them. The first is a quick read with all the pertinent details highlighting exciting changes in our business such as new clients, new offerings, and growth in our business. It always includes a quote from me or a client to add interest and integrity.

The shorter release gets posted to the online PR services sites and submitted to print publications. Because it's so easy to skim, it's often published and read. It meets our goal to increase our visibility.

The second release is a longer version with more details. This one is posted to our website. When it relates to client work we've done, we write a paragraph about the project and include a client quote along with a quote from me. We frequently use this version for offers and testimonials.

Focus on your target market. Write releases that appeal to your target market. Highlight clients you're assisting in your micro-segment. Mention their objectives in working with you and the results they achieved. Include a quote that reinforces the value they've found in your efforts together.

Use these releases to gain credibility in your target group. Once you've issued a press release you can freely quote your clients and their results as a testimonial.

Publish others' releases. There will be times when you are included in other people's press releases. Post them to your website and release them to your media network as well. Mention in another company's release extends your credibility and visibility even further than when you issue a release.

Press release frequency guidelines. The frequency with which you choose to publish releases is a factor of both your resources and your attraction strategy objective. While you may have plenty you can highlight in a press release, you might not have the time or money to do so.

Consider your attraction strategy objective and then align your resources to it. If you need to build your credibility and

become better known across your target segment to successfully close business, publicity is critical. No one is going to buy
from someone they've never heard of, so you need to get your
name out there. In this case, you need to be seen. Issue press
releases every 4–6 weeks. Secure some interviews and publish
a story or two where your micro-segment is sure to spot it.
Highlight new clients in articles and testimonials. Keep at it
for a minimum of six months, ideally a year to 18 months.

If you're already well known but would like to stay visible
to your target market, you needn't be as aggressive. You can
issue press releases once every four months and periodically
interview with journalists. Your other attraction strategies will
probably keep you in front of your prospects, so publicity isn't
as critical to your sales success.

If you drop out of visibility from publicity sources, your
other attraction strategies may not be enough to maintain your
credibility long term. If you choose not to use press releases,
be sure you're seen by your micro-segment in places other than
your own website, emails, and events.

Jump In

Many people are afraid of publicity strategies. Don't be. The
most important thing to remember is that you can do it
yourself or engage companies out there who can do it for you
at reasonable rates. There are numerous tools and resources
available if you want to do it. If you desire the benefit of the
visibility and credibility, but not the added work, engage
someone to do it for you.

As one PR expert said to me, publicity isn't rocket science.
Its tenacity, a few skills, and a database of places to post.

Once you begin using public relations as an attraction strategy, you increase your visibility and credibility across your target market while also providing yourself a repository of educational offers you can leverage with other strategies. Implement this strategy and see how quickly your target market thinks of you as the ubiquitous expert!

When Not to Use Online PR

Publicity strategies are a soft way of building awareness and creating credibility for yourself and your company with your micro-segment. These activities work best over time as your target market is continually exposed to great news items about your company.

These strategies won't necessarily have immediate results. If you're looking for short-term pipeline-filling results PR strategies may not be your best attraction method.

They're a great choice if you're trying to build your visibility and credibility as well as awareness for yourself and your company.

Part 4

Pick Your Collaborative Attraction Strategies

Collaborative

Collaborative attraction strategies are those where you engage with others to capture prospects' interest. These are strategies that typically you wouldn't do alone because of the amount of work, such as an event, or the nature of the strategy, such as alliance partnering.

These strategies are a mixture of the personal and digital strategies in that sometimes they can be very controlled and other times they may not be controlled at all. For example, you may collaborate with your team or an alliance partner to run an event. You have the option of choosing if you'd like to limit the invitations to a specific list of prospects in your target market, or you can promote the event through social media and open it up to anyone who decides they want to attend.

If you choose to limit the invitations, you know the profile of the participants. They're part of your target market and you can be certain that the content of your event will be a fit.

If you post the invitation on several social networks, you can't be certain what the profile of the participants will be. Even if you write the invitation to say that the event is specifically for insurance agencies, you may have other people who choose to attend because the topic peaks their interest.

From my perspective it's perfectly okay if people outside your target market respond to your collaborative attraction strategies. The goal of your lead generation is find new prospects that your solutions fit. So, unless you are limited to the insurance target market, you can sell to these new prospects, too! Don't worry that other people outside your target market begin to participate.

Welcome them.

If, after welcoming them, you don't feel your offerings are a good fit, you simply don't follow up unless they contact you directly. If the prospects do contact you directly, refer them to a company that can better assist them.

There are four collaborative attraction strategies.

- **Online events**—including webinars, audiocasts and teleseminars as a cost-effective approach to reach larger, dispersed audiences

- **Local events**—such as lunch-and-learns and executive breakfasts to meet qualified prospects in person, establish credibility and begin relationship building

- **Offline PR**—including traditional public relations to raise awareness for your company and establish its credibility

- **Alliance Partners**—including people and companies you've identified that you'd like to work with to promote, sell or deliver each other's offerings.

Use the tips and tricks in this section to collaborate with others to attract new prospects.

19

Online Events

Events are one of my favorite techniques for attracting prospects because the people who attend already realize they have an issue and are looking for more information to address it. While they haven't necessarily decided if they'll *pay* for assistance, they have determined that they need to fix something. This means they're further along in their buying process so less awareness education is required on our part.

Events are the chance to show how to address an issue or need, how other companies have done it, and where your expertise can help. If you're subtle and avoid blatant product sales demonstrations, you can reap some highly qualified leads before the end of the session.

It used to be that events had to occur in person in the forms of seminars and workshops. In the past several years people have become highly accustomed to attending online events to gather their information. In fact, they've gotten so used to it that they'll sign up for an event knowing they can't attend at the scheduled time but planning to listen to a recording later. And, many of them really do listen at a different time.

This works in your favor because online events are easy and affordable to run. Add to it that once they're recorded you have a tool that you can use over and over as an offer in your lead generation strategies as well as in the sales process. When you consider the continued use aspect, online events more than pay for themselves in a very short period of time.

Why Sellers Shy Away

There are three challenges that cause sellers to shy away from running events, online or in-person.

1. How to get people to enroll
2. The details, logistics, and costs of executing the event
3. How to identify qualified leads

While these challenges can seem daunting, let's break them down into simple steps so you too can use events as a tool to uncover prospects who recognize they need help.

How to Get People to Enroll

When you decide you're going to hold an event, it may feel alarming to think about how you'll get anyone to enroll, but you already have the strategies to do it.

Post it on your website. Your first step is to post the event details and registration page on your website. If you aren't sure where on your site to post it, put it in your News, Resources, or About Your Company section. Include a brief mention about it on the home page. All your electronic invitations will point people to the details on your webpage and anyone who visits your site will see the event.

Promote the event in your email signature line. Mention the event in the tagline of your signature and include a hot link to more details.

Starting Jan. 28: *New sales Master Series* for hiring and lead generation

Join me for fresh *Email PowerProspecting* strategies: Free webinar June 23

Promote it in your newsletter. If you publish a newsletter, use it to promote the event. If you issue it monthly, start talking about the event four or five weeks in advance. Include the link for additional information and registration.

Most people don't sign up for online events until one or two weeks before the date, sometimes even the day before, but those who are very interested may sign up now. For everyone else, you're starting the awareness-building process by letting them know you're going to hold an event on the topic. If they're even remotely interested in attending, they'll acknowledge it and file it away in the back of their mind.

If you publish another newsletter two or three weeks before the event, promote it again. Those people that were pondering attendance may enroll now that it's closer to the date.

Consider sending a series of email invitations to your newsletter subscribers if the majority of them fall within your target market for this event.

Send an email invitation to your micro-segment. In addition to promoting the occasion in your newsletter, send an email invitation to your micro-segment list 10 days before the event. These are the people you're running the event for, so be sure they know about it.

Turn your email invitation into an email campaign. Increase attendance by making your invitation an email prospecting campaign. Use all the techniques of an email prospecting campaign to grab attention and increase enrollment. The personalization of your campaign will show your contacts how interested you are in their participation.

Here's how it works.

1. Begin the campaign three weeks before the event with an email invitation.

2. Send one email invitation reminder two weeks before the event.

3. Send two email invitations the week before the event.

4. Send one last email invitation the day of the event to capture spontaneous participants.

Use subject lines such as "Can you attend?" and "Will you be able to join me?" to increase the probability that your email will garner a response. You'd be surprised how many people will tell you "I have a conflict at that time" or "We're all set in that area." Your goal in prospect attraction is to start a conversation, and these responses allow you to engage with the contact.

Announce it to your social networks. Include a link to the event description and registration page. See the "Use Social Media to Promote Other Attraction Strategies" chapter for tips and tricks. You may be inclined to ignore this step in your event promotion, thinking that it really won't have that significant an impact on attendance, but I've experienced otherwise numerous times.

Recently I was speaking at an event on behalf of another organization. When I checked in the day before the event, the enrollment was dismal. Just 27 people had enrolled. When you consider that less than 40% of enrollees actually attend an event, I was concerned that I'd put all this effort in for 10 people. Because I was a guest and not hosting the event, I wouldn't have the added leverage of re-using the recording. This meant that I was limited to the number of leads I could get from the people who attended or listened later.

So, I started working my social network. I commented on Twitter, Facebook, and LinkedIn throughout the day. I highlighted that the event was free to my followers and friends, of whom the majority are within our target segment.

Enrollment jumped to 58 people in that short space of time. And because I'd focused on my network, we had a 51% participant rate. Of those 51%, 18% expressed interest in learning more about how we can assist them in their lead generation efforts. Now it was worth the time!

Social networking gets results. Use it.

Invite people when you speak with them. We sometimes get so busy using the new promotion tools that we forget this simple tip! Tell your customers and prospects.

Mention it on your voicemail. For the two weeks preceding the event change your voicemail message to subtly promote the event.

> For the week of April 12 I'll be preparing for our upcoming PowerProspecting webinar in between meetings. Please leave a message and I'll return your call just as soon as possible!

Create an email auto-responder. If you're going to be unavailable while you create the presentation slides or prepare the speakers, view it as an opportunity to get the word out. Put an auto-responder on your email similar to the voicemail. Include a link to the Web page with more details and registration information.

Add an enrollment link to your email signature. People really do ready your signature line, especially if you change it frequently. Add a brief line about the event and a link to enroll.

Ask your alliance partners to promote it. Often your event topic is unrelated to anything your alliance partners do so they'll be more than happy to mention it in their newsletters and to their social networks. Be sure to do the same for them.

Event Detail and Logistics Tips and Tricks

With today's technology you can hold online events with minimal resources. Typically events are either audio-only or webcasts.

Audiocasts and teleseminars. These events are held over the phone with no slides to view during the presentation. If you're going to run an audio conference, I recommend you create a handout for people to follow along and to take notes during the session. The handout can be a printed slide set or a written document.

During delivery, use your handout as your guide just as you would a slide set in a webcast.

I like audiocasts because you don't have to create slides and the technology feels less complex when I'm delivering. Once everyone is on the line, I can begin without worrying about changing slides.

However many people like to have something to view while they're listening, and a handout isn't always sufficient for them. Also, there are times when you're presenting something complex and you'd like the ability to use the webinar tools to direct people's attention. With audio you're limited to your ability to describe what's on the handout in front of them.

On the plus side, phone-based events feel more intimate. When you're going to have a small group of 5–15 and leave the lines open for discussion, it feels more like a meeting than an event. People engage with you and the content and you quickly establish a personal connection with them.

Audio works well for any size audience. With a very large audience you'll want to leave the phone lines muted until it's time for questions. With a small audience, you can leave the lines open for discussion throughout or you can mute them until the question-and-answer period.

Webcasts, webinars, and web seminars. These events have visual slides as well as voice. They can be held where participants watch your slides via the Web and listen in on the phone, or they both watch and listen over the web.

When you anticipate large numbers of attendees, using a full Web-based technology can be more economical because often there is no additional charge for people who listen over the Web. There may be a charge or maximum capacity for additional participants on a telephone conference line, for example 100 people. Typically the capacity for listening over the Web is much higher, say 1,000–2,000.

An added bonus with a webcast is that you can use the tools to help your listeners follow along. Some webinar technologies allow you to integrate surveys, share desktops, and write on the slides.

Interactive tools keep your participants engaged and focused on you. But they also require practice to gain your confidence in using them while you're delivering the event. Many people choose not to use them until they gain experience in delivering webinars.

Choose a simple host technology. Regardless of whether you select an audio- or Web-based event, choose a host technology that you'll be comfortable with during delivery.

For your first events, you may elect to use your company conference line or a free audio service such as www.freeconferencecall.com. It's free, just like its name, and can be recorded from your phone keypad. They send you an email with an audio download link after the event.

As you get more sophisticated, you may want to be able to manage the recording, see who's on the line, and allow them to post questions. Consider a service such as www.InstantTeleseminar.com.

For webinars www.GoToMeeting.com or www.GoToWebinar.com are very popular and easy to use.

All of these are inexpensive technologies to implement online events. None require additional hardware or software and each is simple to set up. These are just a few of the many technologies available to you today.

Plan to record. People today expect that if they can't attend an online event they can listen to a published recording later, so plan to record your events. You may choose to limit them to listening from a web link and not a download, but still be sure to provide a recording.

One benefit to audio recordings is that you receive an MP3 or MP4 format. This means your participants can download the recording and listen to it anywhere they are: At the gym, in the car, at work. They aren't limited to listening when they have a Web connection to view the slides as well.

Several companies allow you to publish a webinar in a downloadable format. If you plan to do this, remember to describe information on slides as you would with an audio delivery. This way people who aren't following the slide will understand your content, too.

Determine the appropriate length. Traditionally online events have been 60 minutes in length. With people's schedules getting tighter and tighter we've seen some that are 30 minutes and others that go 90 minutes.

Typical online events include content delivery followed by a question-and-answer period. Whatever length you choose, reduce it by 10–30 minutes to incorporate participant questions. The length of your question-and-answer period is dependent upon the number of questions you anticipate participants will have.

The value of the content to your micro-segment really determines the length. If you want to supply a few timely tips, then keep it short. If your topic is an industry-changing trigger event, extend it to 90 minutes.

The average online event today is between 45 and 60 minutes.

Carefully choose your time of day (or night). It used to be critical to choose a time of day when the majority of your micro-segment would be available. With the ability to record events this has become less important to the people hosting and attending.

Still, you want as many people to attend live as possible. You'll have more interesting questions for the recording. And increased attendance demonstrates interest in your topic.

Stick to Tuesdays, Wednesdays, or Thursdays. Mondays are often hectic with internal meetings and Fridays are days to wrap things up before the weekend.

Watch for specific times of the month that may be more difficult. For example, sellers on monthly quotas don't want to attend an event at the end of month or quarter. CPAs won't attend events during tax season.

Choose a time of day when you know most of your target segment tends to be available. Lunchtime is still the most popular time of day, between 11:00 A.M.–1:00 P.M. Some single proprietors may prefer evening events between 5:00 P.M.–7:00 P.M.

If you expect that you'll have participants from all over the world and you're based in North America, 11:00 A.M.–1:00 P.M. Eastern works well for European participants. Evenings work best if you plan on having Asian participants.

Use your knowledge of your target market to determine the most appropriate time for your events.

How to Identify Qualified Leads from Your Event

Your objective in holding an event is to attract prospects who already recognize they have a need and are looking for ways to address it. Some people who attend are in their early information-gathering stage and aren't ready for a sales call. Some appreciate the information you've shared and want to try to solve it on their own. Others heard what you had to say and want to know more about how you might assist them.

This third group is the one we want to identify quickly.

Set up offer registration pages. Before the event, choose a way to capture the names of people who would really like to learn more about how you can help them. To entice people to go to these pages make an offer related to the event content, for example, an article, checklist or copy of the slides. (See the next chapter, "Attract Prospects with your Expertise at Events" for more on using offers at events.)

Ideally you'd like to establish an offer registration page on your Web site. Here's how it works.

The registration page requires participants to fill in their name, email address, and any other information you include to receive the offer. To comply with the spam laws, they receive an email asking them to confirm their request. Upon request they are directed to a Web page with the offer ready for download, or they receive another email with a link to that Web page.

The registration page is similar to what you probably already require for people to sign up for your newsletter, if you have one.

Enhance your offer registration page. A registration page alone won't help you identify which contacts want to speak with you right now. You need to enhance it slightly to gather this information.

I recommend adding a check box that says, "I am interested in learning more about . . ."

So, if you're holding an event on how to establish a business interruption plan, the check box might read: "I am interested in learning more about your business interruption services."

Anyone who chooses this box is a lead you want to call within 24 hours of the event.

Adapt the registration concept. If you don't have registration page capability, plan to ask participants to send you an email requesting that you send them the offer. Use your response to them as an opportunity to begin a discussion and to set a follow-up appointment.

Your website may have even more levels of sophistication that allow you to see the names of visitors to your offer Web page. In this case you won't need a registration page but you still want a way for them to indicate their higher degree of interest. Determine how you can have them do so. It may be a follow-up email or another type of offer that only very qualified prospects would want.

Consider Outside Assistance

As you can see, events are an excellent source of qualified leads. If you like the idea of using them as one of your attraction strategies but are tepid about it consider the resources you can engage.

Alliance Partners. Often you'll have alliance partners or peers who use events as part of their lead generation strategy. Consider co-hosting an event, being a guest speaker, or simply asking for advice for your first one.

Vendors. In many industries, such as manufacturing, financial services and information technology, companies resell other companies' products. In these situations the vendors of your products often have resources to speak at your events, invitations you can tailor, or even slides you can deliver as your own. Investigate these options and leverage what you can to reduce your efforts.

Outside resources. Time is at a premium and you may prefer to engage a professional to host your event and manage the recording. You or another person act as the expert and deliver the content, but someone else is on the line to ensure there are no technical difficulties, manage in-bound questions during the session, and create the final recording.

These approaches allow you to begin using events without assuming responsibility for all the details associated with them.

When Not to Use Online Events

Events you're hosting generally require a minimum of 30 days to plan. You want to be sure to give people enough advance notice so they can plan to attend. This means you need to begin promoting it three weeks before the scheduled date. Before sending the invitation you must choose the topic, write a compelling invitation, secure the speaker and set up however you'll take registrations. After the invitation is sent, you must prepare the presentation slides, educational offer, and offer registration page.

With all these activities, most events require six to eight weeks to plan and execute effectively. If you need leads immediately, you'll want to hold off using online events.

20

Attract Prospects with Your Expertise at Events

· · · · · · · · · · · · · · · · · ·

Getting people to attend your event is only half the equation of attracting prospects. The other half is providing an occasion from which they receive useful information. This means your event must be packed with high-quality information important to your target market.

This can occur both during and after the event. During the event, your content and expertise grab them. Afterward it's your offer and follow-up campaign.

During the Event

There are four things participants want when they attend an event, and you have to be able to provide it with your content.

What Participants Want	What to Provide
1. To **Learn** something new about the topic that drew their participation	Provide additional details on the topic. Focus on the trigger events and business aspects. Avoid discussing anything that resembles product solutions or demonstrations.
2. To **Discover** something they did not previously know about a different topic	Give a twist on the business issue at hand, another way to think about it, something they hadn't considered before, or other business issues that may arise from the main topic.
3. To **Know** facts and new information	Here you might include a case study, a customer speaker, a reference, or statistics from a recent analysis.
4. To **Understand** how to address what they have just discovered and learned	Make recommendations to address the trigger event or business issue based on your expertise and offerings.

Notice that people don't come for a product demonstration. They come to learn from you so they can determine what their appropriate next steps should be. It's your knowledge and expertise they want.

Give your expertise freely. Many sellers are concerned about giving away too much knowledge, especially those in service industries. They're afraid that if they disclose too much about how to address a particular issue their prospects won't need their help and competitors will steal their intellectual property.

While there are people who will attend your events and be able to take action based on the information you've provided, there will also be those who can't or don't want to. These are your real prospects.

The people who plan to do it themselves were never opportunities for you, anyway. If questioned, they'd likely tell you that they don't use outside resources. They have internal organizations in place instead.

Don't let these "do-it-yourselfers" detract you from providing your true prospects valuable information for their decision-making process. Eventually the "do-it-yourselfers" may reach a point when they need your assistance and they'll call you because you freely gave of your expertise.

Know what expertise they need. With only an hour to present, you can't begin to tell your micro-segment attendees all they need to know on a given topic. Identify what's most critical and interesting for them.

I typically choose one topic, then offer a lot of information about it. I've found this is much more rewarding to participants than giving just a smattering of information across a broad topic. It also allows me to demonstrate my depth of expertise.

Integrate case studies and demonstrate credibility. Case studies, scenarios, and stories of clients you've worked with help listeners envision a situation and a possible solution. They also add credibility to you and your company.

When you incorporate a case study, include:

- The issue or need your client was facing.

- The strategy your contact employed to address the issue and how you assisted.

- A timeline documenting the phases or steps.

- Any challenges you or your customer encountered and how you overcame them.

- What changed in your client's business after the issue was addressed.

- A quote or testimonial, if you have one.

When a case study doesn't fit in your event, intersperse a few stories about customers you've worked with, challenges they were grappling with, and how you helped them.

If you're concerned about giving away too much intellectual property, case studies allow you to provide valuable information while limiting how much content you actually provide. When you limit content, expect that participants will ask questions to fill in gaps in their own minds. While you always want to answer their questions completely, you won't have any intellectual property on a slide that they can copy.

Case studies and stories not only demonstrate your credibility, they also invite leads. Those in your micro-segment hear examples of customers you've worked with, challenges they've encountered, how you've assisted customers overcome the challenges, and suddenly their interest in working with you peaks. You don't have to brag. Simply relating the story will be enough.

Demonstrations can work in events. There will be times when you want to integrate a demonstration of a product or process from your offerings into an event. You must be extremely cautious not to turn the event into a sales demonstration or you'll alienate everyone who attended.

To do this, use brief clips, screen shots, or actual demonstrations to emphasize a key point about the topic. Show it from the perspective of "this is how one client did it." Or, "this is what we do in our system."

Show the demonstration quickly, then move back into the valuable content about the topic at hand. This approach to a demonstration reinforces a key point in the presentation while establishing your credibility. For those participants who are considering solving their own need, their interest will be piqued but not satisfied. They'll want to schedule a meeting to learn more. For others who aren't as interested, the demonstration will be brief enough not to detract from the value of the rest of the presentation.

Remember that you can always include an option on the offer registration page for people to request a demonstration. That will allow those people who want to learn more to say so.

Create "seed" questions. If your online event isn't interactive, and many are not, leave time at the end for questions and use the "seed" questions that you've prepared in advance if necessary.

Here's my rule of thumb.

Event Length	Q&A Time Period
90 minutes	20–25 minutes
1 hour	15 minutes
30 minutes	7–10 minutes

The question-and-answer period is participants' opportunity to ask you, the expert, for your advice. If you've provided valuable information to them throughout the presentation they'll have burning questions and you want to allow sufficient time for everyone to ask them.

Sometimes your prospects are reluctant to ask the first question. To jumpstart the requests, have three or four "seed" questions at hand. These are typical inquiries you're always asked about the topic but didn't cover in the presentation.

Launch them easily with "I just received a question via email from Tom." Or, "Sally from Minnesota just wrote in . . ."

If you're on an audio conference, give people time to think of their questions by starting with, "I often get asked about . . ." Then answer it while they're thinking.

Prepare your audience for the Q&A period. You know you're going to give attendees the opportunity to ask questions so tell them at the beginning.

Let them know approximately what time you'll be stopping for questions. Encourage them to write down their inquiries as they have them so they don't have to remember them later.

In some online event systems participants can submit their questions as they come up. If you're using a technology like this, invite participants to do so. You can answer them during the event, or hold them to the end.

Attract leads with offers. At every event, include an educational offer that'll entice participants to visit the registration page on your website. Until they complete that page you have no way of gauging their interest.

- Offer a copy of the slides in electronic format, one or two articles, or a checklist related to the session topic. I generally offer three things as well as a free subscription to our weekly tip and monthly e-newsletter.

- Don't forget to include your newsletter if you have one!

- Invite them to connect with you on LinkedIn, Facebook and Twitter.

Mention the offer at the beginning of the event so people know about it. In a webinar where they're just watching slides, this is especially valuable because they won't have to take copious notes if they have access to them later.

When you're talking about something related to the offer, mention it again. For example, "I've included an assessment on the download page to help you determine which of your technical staff are best suited to selling."

For webinars, include the address for the registration page on several slides throughout your presentation. Participants will see it and have the opportunity to write it down or go the page while you're talking.

For audio events, include the address in attendees' handout on the first and last pages with a list of the resources you've included in the event.

At the end of the presentation, repeat the offer and the registration page Web address.

At all my events I offer what we call electronic tools. Each of our events integrates into the presentation some type of tool people can use to do their job better such as an assessment, checklist or customer call action plan.

I offer these tools free of charge to attendees. Because I do it at every event and have done so for many years people who have attended previous events expect them. They've incorporated our tools into their business and now come to my sessions to receive them. Over time these same contacts become clients.

Put some meat on your slides. Lately the trend is to use slides with lots of pretty pictures and not much text. This is fun when you're presenting but doesn't serve well as an offer. It also doesn't reinforce your expertise.

People like to see tables, charts, diagrams, and data. Insert a few slides or pages with valuable information they won't have seen before. Now they'll want a copy when you offer them.

How many people do you really need to be successful?

The goal of your event is to attract qualified prospects who have a need you can address now. While it's rewarding to have 1,000 participants at an event, the odds are that you can't follow up with all 1,000. Even if we say only 10% are leads, that's still 100 people you need to call and move through your pipeline.

Your purpose is to uncover qualified prospects in your micro-segment in manageable numbers. With this objective in mind, you may not need even 40 attendees.

I've run sessions with only eight people. When they're the right eight prospects, that's all that counts. The better refined your target segment and the topic of your event, the higher your quality of participants will be. Determine what number you require in attendance to achieve your goal.

Because online events are inexpensive, no travel is required and the recordings can be leveraged as offers for other prospect attraction strategies. You don't need large numbers of people attending to see a return on your investment.

Keep in mind that once you've designed the event, you can also run it multiple times if you choose.

After the Event

After your event there are three groups of people you may choose to follow up with.

1. Participants who expressed interest in learning more about you and are leads.

2. Participants who requested the offer but aren't leads.

3. Enrollees who didn't attend.

Of course you'll want to call everyone who is a lead and schedule an appointment. Contact them within 24 hours of the event.

If you're hungry for leads, don't stop there. Plan an email campaign to follow up with the participants who requested the offer but aren't leads.

Your offer to this group is a discussion around any questions they have from the event or the event offer. Because they heard you speak and you've gained credibility with them you may want to have a conversation to gauge their interest.

Not all qualified prospects will indicate their interest on the registration page. This email campaign is designed to uncover them.

Finally, you definitely want to launch an email campaign to the people who enrolled but didn't participate. Include the recording link as your offer. In the email also mention the additional resources you recommended in the event.

Continue the campaign with a follow-up to see if they have questions they'd like to discuss.

Leverage the Recording. After the event, use the recording as an offer for people who didn't enroll. Run an email campaign inviting them to listen.

Split webcasts into smaller podcasts. If your content lends itself, create brief podcasts from the webcast and use them as offers for other prospect attraction strategies. These can be great teasers for people who didn't attend the webcast, too.

21

Local Events

⬤ ⬤ ⬤ ⬤ ⬤ ⬤ ⬤ ⬤ ⬤ ⬤ ⬤ ⬤ ⬤ ⬤ ⬤ ⬤ ⬤ ⬤

Local events are still quite popular. In fact, we have a significant number of clients who host lunch-and-learns, executive breakfasts, open houses, and even afternoon snack sessions. (Notice the food theme. Refreshments are a draw!)

These events provide you an opportunity to meet qualified prospects in person, establish credibility and begin relationship building. You can mingle with participants before and after, asking questions about their situations and answering their questions. During these informal discussions you can quickly qualify a prospect and maybe even set a follow-up meeting.

All this conversation, bonding and qualifying happens before and after the actual event. During the event you can listen to the questions people ask, what peaks their interest, and what finds them checking their emails and texts. This offers you another opportunity to qualify individual participants and determine the appropriate next steps with each one.

Local events are especially successful in areas where there is a strong sense of community. In these areas people like to work with other companies in their area. They want to hear about each other's successes. They'll come to local events to get acquainted with potential providers and hear peer's success stories.

These events typically last longer than an on-line event. Someone who drives to participate expects to be there at least 90 minutes and maybe as long as three hours.

Many of the tips and tricks in the previous two chapters apply to local events. This chapter includes some additional considerations when you're hosting a local event.

Live Events Tips and Tricks

Keep events small. Limit local events to between eight and 40 people. Fewer than eight participants is uncomfortable for many people who may feel captive in a one-on-one sales call. With more than 40 people, you can't spend time with each of them.

Call the list in advance. Because local events are more involved than online ones, you want to be sure you have sufficient numbers of people to attend and that you'll achieve your minimum enrollment. If you have the resources, plan to call the list you'll be inviting before you send out invitations.

When you call, tell people about the event so they'll expect the invitation and consider attending. If you're making the calls yourself, treat this as an opportunity to uncover immediate needs. You may find some leads in your calls even though that's not your objective.

Call your list at least two weeks before sending the invitations.

The invitations. Not long ago invitations to seminars or on-site events were very formal. Today, invitations can be as simple as an email or as formal as a wedding invitation.

However you send it, make sure it's received a minimum of three weeks before the event. Local sessions require people to schedule time out of the office. You want to give them sufficient notice to arrange their calendar to attend.

You may want to send a "save the date" email for important or expensive events.

Always include a Web link to more details about the event and multiple ways for prospects to reply and accept: Phone, email, and online registration. If your target market doesn't frequent the Internet, include a phone and fax number for responses.

Provide directions. While we all can get directions off the Web, your prospects are busy people. Make it as easy as possible for them to attend. On the registration page include a link to quickly download directions from their location to the event location. You can also include directions with a visual map on the registration page or with the invitation.

Plan to follow up with everyone you've invited. If you have email addresses, create an email invitation follow-up campaign. If not, call those who haven't enrolled and personally invite them. Begin your follow-up campaign and calls five to seven days after the invitations have been mailed. Typically you want to call three to five business days before an on-site event.

These touches serve not only as a reminder to contacts about the event but also as another encouragement to attend.

Comment about it. Even though you've sent out invitations to personally invite people, use your social network to get the word out and increase attendance.

Be prepared to host your guests. Executive breakfasts and luncheons are always appreciated. Even with mid-morning or afternoon events, refreshments are expected. Be prepared to invest in food and beverages to make your guests comfortable.

Use information request forms. While you can use registration pages to capture leads from local events, this actually is more difficult for your participants than when they're attending an online event. They have to remember to go back to the office and log in to request the offer.

If they have a mobile phone with Internet access on hand, they can do it during the session. Otherwise, we're asking attendees to work harder than we want them to.

Instead of using an online registration page, use a paper information request form. The content is similar, but this is something they can complete at their leisure during the event. (If your group is large or prefers technology, you can use both a registration page and an information request form and leave it up to individuals to choose which they use.)

Hand it out with any session materials when participants arrive and retrieve it as they leave. Then email them a link to the download page the day after the session.

I like information request forms because you can gather more intelligence than on a registration page. People are so immune to online registration forms that they have no tolerance for inputting much data. We have to keep them very short.

With an information request form that's provided at the beginning of the session, participants have an hour or longer to complete it. We can ask things such as what they liked best about the session and what topics would they be interested in at future events.

On our form I even ask for a referral!

While you do have to manually email every person who requests the offer download page link, the additional information you gather is priceless.

Include a give-away. One of the benefits of local events is the opportunity to get contacts' business cards. Their cards provide titles, direct phone numbers, correct spelling of names, and email addresses.

To be sure you get everyone's card, include a give-away in your session. Books, free product, and even T-shirts get people excited.

I try to give away something related to the session and of value. Because I'm an author, I'll give away copies of my book. But when the book subject doesn't relate to the event topic, I choose other items such as a sales manager assessment or seats at an upcoming audio conference of their choice. These are items people really want and they'll stay until the end of your session to see if they've won.

When Not to Use Local Events

Unlike online events, local ones can be costly. Typically they require an investment in food or coffee, tea, soda and juice. Many times you'll also be paying for printed invitations, postage, and hotel space.

They can also be risky. If only a handful of people attend, you don't have the benefit of a recording to reuse as an offer. You'll spend a lot of time and money and may not get any leads.

If you're operating on a shoestring budget or within a limited time period, local events may not be the best approach for you.

22

Off-line PR

I n the *Online PR* chapter we looked at different ways you can leverage the Internet to promote yourself, your business, and your offerings. Often people think that's the only type of public relations they can afford or have the skills to do. Now let's look at how people who have limited funds, limited time, and limited skills can use traditional publicity to build credibility, extend their visibility, and attract customers, too.

The good news for you is that reporters are always looking for news. Every day they have to find new, exciting information to print or televise. So each day presents a new opportunity for you to get publicity.

Offline PR Tips and Tricks

Just be seen. If you're a small business in a local community, it can be easier to get the attention of the press. Local papers want to focus on businesses in their area, highlighting successes they're having, so start there. When you hire or promote people, send out a quick two-sentence notice. If you launch a new offering, send another brief note. Forward your short press release like we discussed in *Online PR.* Call when you've done something significant.

Use the headline news. Even if you don't have an exciting new product or client you can use to catch a reporter's attention, you may be able to piggyback off today's national news and give a local comment.

Watch the headline stories in local and national news that affect your target market. Whatever is on the front page of the newspaper in the morning will probably be on the TV news that night, providing you an opportunity for publicity.

Call the local TV station or newspaper and offer a comment with local perspective. The next thing you know, they'll be sending a crew over to tape you for the 11:00 news or writing your statement to print. Or, if you have video recording capability through your phone or a Flip camera, record a brief segment and send it to the station. Now you've made it extra easy for them to post on their website.

Secure a spot on a local radio talk show. Listen to your local media and see what the business radio show is talking about. If you have something relevant, call them with your idea. Think of topics they may not yet have covered but that would interest their listeners.

They're always looking for new people to interview because there's an unending supply of air time on the radio.

Study the publication's audience. If you've identified a publication you know you simply must be seen in, study its audience. Become an active reader. Send them the types of articles you know their readers will appreciate. Call and offer comments on articles. Make yourself available for quotes.

Sell to local reporters. Just as you want to network with journalists on-line, you should do the same with local editors and reporters. Get to know them and start pitching feature ideas about your company, expert quotes, or articles.

Be careful not to take advantage of your relationship by sending too many ideas at once. Save only the best concepts to pitch. When you offer too many suggestions, especially if they're not good ones, you could sour a contact against you.

Focus on a niche of reporters. It's better to call on four reporters who are definitely interested in your expertise than it is to call on 15 who really aren't. Segment reporters just as you do prospects. Identify those who write within your target market: Insurance, health care and finance, or the community you serve.

Establish a relationship with them. Become the recognized expert they can turn to for a quick quote or interview and for referrals to others they can quote.

As your relationship strengthens, they'll refer you to other journalists and even accept average story ideas.

Get a story written about your company. You don't have to be a $15 million company or have the most exciting offerings in the world to have a feature written about your company. Use the success of your business to entice the local business reporter. If you've grown dramatically, launched an interesting new product, received a prestigious award, or made a significant charitable contribution, journalists will be interested.

Grab Reporters' Attention

Catching the attention of a reporter is a lot like prospecting. You have to call and pitch your idea in 30 seconds or less. Here are four quick steps to success.

1. When the journalist answers, be direct and say that you're calling to pitch a story idea that might be of interest.

2. Check to see if this is a good time to call. Reporters are busy people. If they're under a deadline, now won't be the best time. Demonstrate respect for their schedule.

3. If it's a good time, give just enough information to gauge their interest. As in cold calling, avoid dumping too much information on reporters. Catch their attention and make them what to hear more.

4. Ask if the concept interests them, then wait for their answer. If they like it, they'll schedule an interview. If not, thank them for their time. Ask if there are any particular stories they are looking for at the moment. If there's one that fits your experience, tell them. If not, promise to call again when you have another idea you think they'd appreciate.

These strategies are quite successful in small-medium sized markets. If you're targeting the New York Times or Wall Street Journal, you have to have a big concept to get their notice.

Create a Credibility Book

Just as you have a Wall of Fame on your website, you want to promote your offline publicity success. Add print quotes and article citations on your website and create a Credibility Book filled with customer testimonials for the office, too.

This is your Wall of Fame in print.

Strategically position your Credibility Book on the coffee table in your reception area. As prospects wait to meet with you they'll pass their time perusing it.

One client of ours has a thick three-ring binder filled with customer testimonials dating back more than 14 years. There are current letters demonstrating that they're a strong organization and older letters that prove the level of experience their firm brings to the business.

Do the same. Start gathering testimonials from delighted customers. Include them in your Credibility Book. Afterwards turn them into press releases and case studies.

A customer testimonial can be as brief as a quarter of a page. The fact that they wrote, signed, and sent it is what makes the difference. If it came through in email print it and add it to the book. How you received it isn't as important as what they said.

To adapt it to a case study you need more information detailing the original situation, how you solved it, and how you helped their business. All this information can be gathered during one of your regular review meetings or sales calls.

When Not to Use Off-line PR

As with online publicity strategies, offline publicity strategies are focused on building awareness and creating credibility over time. If you need leads immediately, this isn't the best attraction strategy to use.

23

Alliance Partners

· · · · · · · · · · · · · · · · · ·

While you can execute all the activities surrounding prospect attraction yourself, why not enlist some help from others who are working within the same target market? You probably already tap these contacts for referrals. Now go a step further and consider how you can integrate them as a prospect attraction strategy.

Leveraging alliance partners gets other people involved in creating awareness for you and your offerings, especially if they're already engaged with your micro-segment. It reduces the amount of work you have to, and potentially expands your reach to contacts you don't yet have in your target market list.

This is particularly important when you are breaking into a new market where you've never sold before. You don't yet have references, but aligning yourself with sellers already respected by its members often gives you instant credibility.

What's an Alliance Partner?

Alliance partners are those individuals and companies where you jointly decide to work together to promote, sell or deliver each other's offerings. There's a win-win for both of you.

Some organizations limit themselves to only working with alliance partners with whom they have a contractual arrangement. All the arrangements have been defined legally and include some type of an incentive to work with you and your company.

These are the easiest partners to work with because they're motivated by a defined compensation plan. You don't need to sell them on the value of teaming to participate in your prospect attraction programs. They're happy to help you drive leads!

But what if you don't have any contractual arrangements with other companies just yet?

The good news is that there are all sorts of people you can view as your alliance partners. From my perspective, these relationships stem from a state of mind.

Your objective is prospect attraction. That means your name has to be in front of as many people in your micro-segment as possible using as many avenues as are available. Teaming with other people extends your reach into their networks, just as it does with social networking. The difference here is that the two of you have a discussion about specifically how you can assist each other in your attraction efforts.

With social networking all your contacts need to do is "retweet" you. With alliance partnering, you go a step further to share referrals, actively promote each other, and possibly engage in joint prospect attraction strategies.

Step beyond the contractual relationships and consider some of these, too.

Find someone with complementary solutions. A partner may be someone with solutions that are complementary to your own where you're both selling to the same target market and possibly the same contacts. Maybe you sell computer systems and they sell telephone systems.

We align with a company that sells sales skills assessments for leaders, managers, and sellers. We didn't want to create them so we found someone who had them. We pass referrals and even resell them.

Together we've conducted joint webcasts on the importance of assessing and developing your sales staff. We each invite contacts from our micro-segments and leverage our expertise to drive more opportunities to our companies.

Find someone with shared goals. A partner can also be a person who has goals similar to yours and thereby obtains success in the same manner as you. This type of partner is motivated to work with you because you're focused on similar goals. These contacts may be people you network with in leads groups, associations, clubs, or other networks to which you belong. They may also be people you've met in your social networking.

Look to your competitors. It used to be that you'd never talk with your competitors, but now we all recognize that there are times when you may engage your competition to fulfill a gap in your own capabilities. Align yourself with your honest and ethical competitors who aren't selling in your same micro-segments.

I regularly pass leads to another sales consulting organization that has expertise with companies over $100M in annual revenue in service and retail industries. Our area of expertise is with companies under $100M in annual revenue with a specialization in the information technology industry. We both offer sales training programs but for very different target markets. When she has computer industry leads, she passes them to me. It has been such a fruitful relationship that the owner and I now meet on a quarterly basis to share ideas to grow our businesses.

Don't forget your own organization. One of my favorite places to find partners is within our own consulting and service staff. These people are talking with your customers every day. They can listen for leads and even ask a few questions to qualify opportunities for you.

When I worked for IBM, those of us in sales knew that the people who performed maintenance on customers' hardware were excellent sources of customer information. They knew what was happening in the account, heard sidebar conversations, and even spent time around the water cooler chatting with key decision-makers. The information they provided frequently led to new opportunities in those accounts.

You may need to explain what they should listen for or ask, but once your consultants or engineers know what you're seeking they'll become an ideal lead supplier for you.

Alliance Partnering Tricks and Tips

As you can see, contracts aren't required to establish alliance partnerships. There are many levels of partnering that you can employ and over time you'll probably discover that you're using all of them and a bunch I haven't mentioned.

This section includes some ideas on how to maximize these relationships and attract prospects to you both.

Set up informal arrangements. Have a discussion where you agree how you'll support each other. Will you pass leads, comment about each other's blog posts, promote one of their webcasts, or do something more?

This level of discussion may not occur in your first conversation. Often you need time to get to know each other, observe how you serve customers, and learn what your true areas of expertise are. That's okay. In fact, I advise it. This way you can be sure that the person is someone you'll be successful working with. If you jump in too quickly you may regret it.

Pass leads. It has to start somewhere, so why not with you? Once you pass a lead, the trust increases significantly and suddenly your partners will want to do the same for you.

Remember them when you're selling. Listen for opportunities that fit your alliance partner's profile of an ideal prospect. Don't stop listening to a new contact just because there isn't a fit. Wait long enough to see if you can refer him to one of your partners.

Run joint prospect attraction strategies. Maybe you can do a webcast together like I did with the sales assessment company. You could share a booth at a trade show or offer to assist in each other's booths.

You might execute a combined email prospecting campaign. You send the emails to your micro-segment and they send to theirs. The offer is an article that fits needs both your organizations meet in separate manners. Or there could be two offers. If the prospect clicks one, he becomes a lead for you. If he clicks the other, he's a lead for your partner.

There are many ways to leverage your relationship. Look for ways that share the prospect attraction effort.

Be guests on each other's blogs, podcasts, or radio shows. Interview each other. Write articles together. These serve as valuable offers while extending your reach beyond your own list.

Recently I was interviewed by the owner of a web-hosting company who had been asked by his clients to recommend a referral program they could post on their websites to attract more referral leads. Derek and I had been talking about how we could work together but hadn't yet figured it out. His customers afforded us the perfect opportunity.

I was able to give Derek ideas to recommend to his clients and we put them into a series of articles that we now both use as prospect attraction offers, each for different purposes. He shows clients how to implement a referral program on their web site using his company's services. I train them how to create a referral program as part of their sales and implementation process.

Use each other's marketing materials. No need to recreate what already exists. Pool articles, email campaigns, even event presentations to use as a starting point for your attraction strategies. If you wait to create something new, you may never get your fabulous plan launched.

Share lists. If you're selling to the same micro-segment you can share lists without ever passing actual data. In today's sales world, you send your alliance partner's email campaign or special offer to your subscriber list. As people are interested they'll click through to your partner's site and complete their registration form or sign up.

Periodically publish one of your partner's articles. This saves you the energy of writing one and brings fresh content and ideas to your target market.

Your prospects love it because you're providing them good information they may not otherwise have seen. As the expert, your micro-segment appreciates you doing so. Their perception of you actually increases.

Agree on how you'll share leads. If you run joint lead generation activities, agree in advance about how you'll handle contacts that could use both your services.

Set up a referral-passing percentage. If you're a business owner you're in the unique position of earning real revenue for the referrals you give. Establish a referral passing percentage that you each earn on referrals. Now you can share in each other's successes and there's a monetary reward if your partner closes a lead you provided.

Use alliance partnerships to expand into areas of your micro-segment you have yet to reach, even those you may not have been aware of. Use them, too, to reduce your prospect attraction efforts while increasing awareness and leads in your target market.

Now who doesn't want to do that?

When Not to Use Alliance Partners

I can't think of a reason not to use some form of alliance partnering. No matter what you are selling, you can always leverage relationships with other people in your prospect attraction efforts.

Part 5

Pull It All Together

Now I've got you excited! You've chosen the prospect attraction strategies that feel most comfortable to you from the Attraction Trifecta. You know which micro-segments you want to hit first. But you still aren't quite sure how it all comes together to get contacts to respond to you.

Let's clear up the last bit of mystery and look at what a prospect attraction campaign looks like when you combine different strategies.

It may appear complex when you first look at it, but it's really very simple. You've seen each component of it throughout the book. Now I'm pulling it together for you into a campaign.

I've used campaigns just like you'll see here in my own selling activities and I can tell you with confidence that they work. I no longer do any cold calling. I use prospect attraction strategies to generate all the leads we need.

I know you can be as successful as I am. You're ready to do this. Let's go!

24

Choosing Your
Attraction Strategies

O ver the course of this book I've offered you 14 attraction strategies from the Attraction Trifecta, combining personal, digital, and collaborative approaches. I wanted to give you many different lead generation strategies so you have choices. Prospects respond to each one, and I've shared with you when to use a particular strategy and when it won't be a fit.

However, remember my advice at the beginning. Choose the attraction strategies that appeal to you and feel most comfortable. Then commit to doing them on a consistent basis. If you aren't comfortable with a particular strategy, or don't believe it will attract prospects for your target market, it will be difficult for you to give it your best effort in execution. Just like an exercise regime, if you don't like it, you won't do it and you won't see any results. So choose attraction strategies you think you'll enjoy and feel confident in your ability to execute.

It's okay to limit yourself to only two or three attraction strategies in the Trifecta. In fact, choosing too many strategies may be difficult to manage. I suggest that you begin with between two and four strategies. As you link them together, they'll be your winning combination.

The most common prospect attraction strategies for sellers to use in their territories today are email and warm calling. Some sales people also use letters, especially when their target market doesn't respond to email. Savvy sales people also use alliance partners and social media.

The most common prospect attraction strategies for companies to attract leads to pass to sales people today are email, events, social media, letters, and post cards. Thought leaders have increased their use of blogs, newsletters, and public relations to attract prospects in unique ways like we discussed.

While these are the most common attraction strategies that doesn't mean you have to follow the pack. Also consider your target market and your resources. When I'm really busy, I'll only execute email campaigns and social media to my target market. I don't attempt to follow up with warm calls. I stay in front of them, nurturing them, then let prospects respond to me when they're ready. Our target market is small and mid-market companies who use email and social media consistently so this approach is successful for me.

Don't feel you need to try every approach. You don't even have to stretch yourself to attempt new ones right away. Use the tips and tricks I've mentioned to refine how you're executing your attraction strategies and improve your results.

If you determine that your response rates aren't increasing even after tweaking them, then do consider some new approaches. It could be that the attraction strategies you prefer aren't ones to which your target market pays attention.

You don't need to use a lot of different strategies to get results. What you need is consistent execution so you're in front of your prospects when a need arises. That way they'll think of you first!

I do encourage you to integrate social networking. If you're not comfortable with it, start slowly, but do get engaged. Companies all over the world are very involved in social media. When you're engaged, you're perceived as current in your industry. If you're absent, your top prospects may wonder about the depth of your leadership and capabilities whether it's relevant or not. Add to it that social networking expands your reach to a broader number of companies in your micro-segment. You'll rarely be able to purchase a list of all the companies in your target market. Social networking allows you to reduce that gap.

With the Internet, social media is easy to add into your campaign mix and quickly increase your response rates. I'll show you how in the campaign examples in this chapter.

Why These Campaigns Work

You may be wondering why these prospect attraction campaigns work when cold calling or previous attempts at email prospecting have not.

They work for three reasons:

1. They're simple enough for you to do in between all your other responsibilities so you can be consistent.

2. They're personal, focused on your micro-segment about trigger events they're already grappling with, and provide a valuable offer related to those same trigger event issues. They're communicated in such a way that your contacts feel as if you're reaching out to only them, not to a group of 15, 50, or 100.

3. They include follow-up. You don't stop with one

email, one comment, or one event. You extend
offers multiple times. Your target market sees
you in numerous places or in the same manner
repeatedly. You don't let long periods of time
lapse between communications.

These three reasons give the appearance of a personal touch
with each member of your group. If prospects have the need
you've identified and are struggling with that trigger event,
they'll respond to one of your many communication attempts.

Over time those in your target market will begin to view
you as an expert who can help. They'll continue to watch and
observe your communications. They may follow you on a
social network, read your newsletter religiously, follow your
blog, or attend events you host.

If companies don't require your assistance today, when
that changes you'll be top of mind with them because of your
continued focus on them and their segment. They'll remember
to call you and feel confident in your ability to assist them.

The Four Critical Elements

Each prospect attraction strategy or campaign you run will
include four critical elements.

1. The strategy, whether it's email, a postcard, a blog
   post, or another of the 14 approaches.

2. The grabber message, based on a trigger event or
   business issue your target market is facing.

3. The enticing offer you'll make that'll elicit a response from contacts experiencing the issue you highlighted in your grabber message.

4. The single call to action asking for a response.

How these four elements are presented varies to fit the prospect attraction approach you're employing. For example, the length of your message will depend on the strategy you choose. With an email or letter, you have more space than with a single 140-character comment in Twitter.

Your offer may be an abbreviated phrase in a tweet or on a postcard, or the complete title on Facebook or in an email.

Your call to action can be a directive "download this article" during an online event or an implied "enroll" on a postcard.

Regardless, each element serves a purpose and you want to be sure to include them in your attraction strategy. Use the tips in the chapter for each attraction strategy to adapt the four prospect attraction elements to your campaign.

25

Multiple Strategies and One Campaign Equal Many Prospects

By now you know that you don't need a degree in marketing to attract prospects. Likewise, you can connect your attraction strategies in simple campaigns and increase response rates. Marketing experts do this all the time. So can you.

There are two distinct types of campaigns you can use:

1. One Message, Multiple Strategies
2. One Strategy, Multiple Messages

"One Message, Multiple Strategies" Campaign

In the "One Message, Multiple Strategies" campaign you use several different attraction strategies all designed to target your micro-segment with the same, specific message. This means that your grabber trigger event is the same throughout the whole campaign, while the attraction strategies you use vary throughout the campaign.

Chris' target market is schools from kindergarten through high school. He's chosen improved student safety as the trigger event and wants to run a campaign using four different attraction strategies, ending with an on-line webinar event. Chris has decided to focus his message throughout the campaign on improved student safety in schools.

In Chris' campaign, notice how the single message, offer, and call to action are consistent across email, social networking, alliance partners, and the on-line webinar event. His campaign begins with two emails and social networking both talking about the same message, improved student safety in schools.

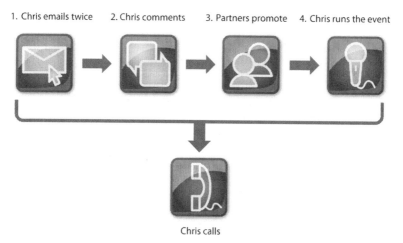

1. Chris emails twice   2. Chris comments   3. Partners promote   4. Chris runs the event

Chris calls

Same trigger event ▪ Same offer ▪ Same call to action

1. The first email discusses the trigger event and mentions the webinar. The second email is an invitation to attend the event, mentioning the trigger event.

2. While the emails are going out, Chris plans to use social networking to comment on both the trigger event and the upcoming prospect attraction event.

3. As the event draws closer, Chris will engage alliance partners to spread the word about the event to their list of contacts in his target market, schools from kindergarten through high school.

4. Chris collaborates with his team to conduct the webinar.

5. The campaign ends with Chris calling the people who enrolled and/or attended. Notice that throughout the campaign Chris calls any leads that he uncovers. Throughout any campaign you run there can be prospects who may not want to wait for the point you've identified as appropriate to call. He plans to encourage these prospects to attend the event, but if they are hot leads, he's going to follow up immediately. Finally, if Chris has the data available, he'll also follow up with people who did not enroll, but clicked to learn more about the event from the emails they received or the social media comments they followed.

Vary your offers. As you continue this type of campaign you could repeat it with the same grabber message reworded and a different offer, such as an article, video segment, or short case study. Your offer to attend an event may not have been of interest to some members of your target market, but the offer to watch a brief podcast might be of interest. Varying the offer will keep your message fresh and interesting. It's a simple way to repeat the campaign and stay present with your micro-segment.

Expand on the trigger event. If you want to run a longer campaign spanning three or four months, you can expand on the trigger event by talking about it from different perspectives. It's still the same trigger event, just with more details or perspective.

Chris decided he'd stretch his campaign over four months. He determined that he could expand on improved student safety to talk about the importance of:

- Protecting students while at school
- Staying in touch with parents about their children's welfare
- Communicating with teachers about individual students
- Building safety measures

You can probably think of several additional perspectives related to student safety, but you get the point. It's just one trigger event.

When to use this approach. If your target market has only one primary trigger that you can address, or that they care about, the "One Message, Multiple Strategies" approach is very effective. You can still use prospect attraction campaigns to uncover leads, but you don't have to try to find lots of different business issues to talk about.

This approach is also useful when you have a lot of different ways to talk about the trigger event or business issue that prospects in your micro-segment may be facing. It keeps you in front of prospects in unique ways that don't appear repetitive.

"One Strategy, Multiple Messages" Campaign

In the "One Strategy, Multiple Messages" campaign you use one attraction strategy and multiple messages. You choose the attraction strategy that is most effective in your target market and most comfortable for you, and use it as the basis for your campaign. You then choose several trigger events or business issues to focus on in the campaign. Often your target market will have at least three trigger events or business issues you can select from.

Deb's target market is restaurant groups. She identified four business issues she frequently sees in her restaurant customers. She believes that prospects in her target market probably struggle with the same business issues.

- Staff retention

- Billing issues

- Inefficient ordering processes

- Catering and take-out expansion opportunities

Rather than choose a single business issue to focus on, Deb wants to highlight each one throughout her campaign. She wants her prospects' responses to the campaign offers show her what their priorities are for their businesses.

Deb is very busy and doesn't have time for an involved campaign. She decided to use email as her primary prospect attraction strategy and then phone calls to follow up on leads. This is how her campaign looks.

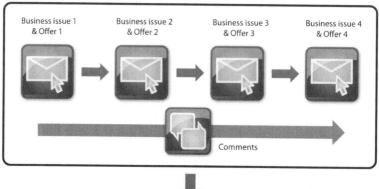

Responses & click-thru's

1. Using the tips from Chapter 8, Create an Email Campaign to Increase Results, each email highlights a different trigger event or business issue and makes an offer related to it. The call to action may be to reply or agree to a meeting.

2. The emails are spaced about two weeks apart so Deb's target market doesn't feel inundated with communications from her.

3. If Deb chooses, she can comment in her social networks about the business issues and include links to the campaign offers. This will extend her reach, but if she doesn't have time to do it and only wants to send email campaigns, she can do that.

4. Throughout the campaign Deb will call anyone who responds. Responses may come as email replies or calls. If her email system has the

capability, she can also call people who click through to the offers.

What if you don't have multiple trigger events? You may find yourself in a situation where you're only comfortable with two attraction strategies, such as email and warm calling, but don't have multiple trigger events you can use for your message. In this circumstance you can use the same business issue but incorporate different offers with each email. To make your emails seem different to prospects, change the way you write about the business issue in each one. With a unique offer accompanying the individual emails, your campaign won't appear repetitive.

This approach works for any of the attraction strategies, not just email.

Earlier in this chapter, the section "Expand on the Trigger Event" can give you more ideas on how to make the same business issue sound different.

When to use this approach. You may be in a situation where after reading this book only one or two prospect attraction strategies feel comfortable to you. Or, your company may only support one or two prospect attraction strategies. Or, you may be time constrained and need to get something started right away. If you find yourself in any of those situations, the "One Strategy, Multiple Messages" approach is the ideal campaign strategy for you to generate leads.

You don't have to mix a bunch of attraction strategies to get leads. Multiple strategies will help to expand your visibility and reach a wider audience in your target market. But what's most important is consistent execution and follow up.

26

What if Prospects Aren't Responding?

Yes, there will be times when your target market is immune to your grabber and your offer. In those instances, there are several places to examine and adjust.

1. Are you targeting an intimate enough group that your prospect attraction strategy can appear to be highly personal? When you execute a lead generation campaign, target group members should be contacts with similar responsibilities and issues. If your target group is not similar enough it will be difficult to create a campaign that feels personal.

2. Do your attraction strategy and grabber feel personal? Evaluate if the attraction strategy you're using is personal enough. For example, a newsletter is not as personal as an email that includes each contact's name. Perhaps you need to begin your campaign with a more personal approach. Evaluate if one of the personal attraction strategies will be more effective with this target market.

If the approach feels right, examine the grabber. To help you to write from a more personal perspective, imagine yourself speaking with a prospect you know from the micro-segment. Write using similar phrases and words as you would if you were talking with that prospect.

3. Is your grabber compelling, related to a key trigger event or primary issue many of the members of your micro-segment are facing? Frequently when prospects aren't responding there is nothing in the message related to their trigger event or issue. The biggest mistake sellers make is to talk primarily about their company and forget to focus on their prospects. Mention your company, but save the majority of what you'd like to share. Use that information in your first appointment or if the prospect responds with questions.

4. Did you include a clear call to action? We know we'd like the prospect to read the blog post we referenced, sign up for the event, or agree to a first meeting. Did you clearly ask the prospect to do it? Be clear about what action the prospect should take.

5. Is there only one call to action so individuals aren't confused about what you're asking them to do? It's enticing to offer several calls to action to increase our perceived value to prospects. However, multiple calls to action have the opposite effect. They only confuse your contacts, causing your response rates to suffer.

6. Is the message concise? If it's too long they won't take the time to read or listen to it.

7. Is your offer enticing to them? A needs analysis is not of value when prospects are just beginning to think about the issue. They need more education about that issue and possibly about your company before they'll agree to you analyzing their situation.

8. Does the title of the offer make it sound interesting and exciting or dry as dust? Sometimes all you need to do is make a minor adjustment, such as changing the title of an offer, to increase your response rates.

9. Are you attempting to communicate with them on a consistent, frequent basis, as often as every three days? While you may be concerned about reaching out too frequently, if your micro-segments only see you once or twice a month they can easily ignore you. If they aren't aware of you, your company or your message, it will be difficult to create awareness without frequent communication. Use multiple attraction strategies to stay visible without overwhelming prospects.

10. Does your micro-segment pay attention to the strategies you're using? You may want to do a bit of research to identify what contacts watch. If they don't check email, email prospecting won't be the best method. If social networking isn't authorized in their company, commenting won't be seen. When you're employing only one or two attraction strategies and not getting any leads, consider doing some research to validate the approach you've chosen.

If your approaches aren't working, use these questions as a checklist to review what you're doing. Adjust and try again.

If your techniques continue to fail, test your attraction strategy with several of your top clients in the same target market. Discuss the trigger events and business issues you've identified. Share the grabber messages and offers you've created. Your top clients value their relationship with you and want to see you succeed. They'll provide you firsthand recommendations on what to change. In fact, if you have time, testing with top clients can give you valuable insight before you invest your resources to launch a campaign.

27

Become a
"Sales Magnet"

N ow you know all my secrets to attract more great prospects without cold calling. You may even have tried some of them firsthand before reading this book. None of the 14 strategies in the Attraction Trifecta are too difficult. Some are more time-consuming than others. Nearly all are relatively easy to do once you get started.

As I close I want to leave you with a challenge. Being the competitive seller that I'm sure you are, I expect you'll take me up on it!

Choose one attraction strategy to try with your target market tomorrow. Don't wait to get a list or to create a campaign. Just do it.

Get Started Now!

You already have a list of prospects you've been meaning to call. You know the one I mean. It's the group in your CRM, or the stack of business cards on your desk. They're the prospects you haven't gotten around to just yet.

They probably all fit into a target market, perhaps by company size or industry. If not, divide it into target markets and pick one. You only may have 10 people, but still, that's a targeted list.

You know your target market's business issues. Pick an offer already on your website, blog, or company server. Then one, two, three, go!

- Start an email campaign.

- Send a personal letter to each contact.

- Plan a lunch-and-learn event to take place in your conference room in three weeks and send out email invitations.

Get visible so others in your target market can get to know you. This will help you quickly expand your list beyond those 10 people.

- Begin commenting on LinkedIn, Twitter or Facebook to be visible.

- Start blogging where your target market pays attention.

Then consider all those other sales people and business owners you've met at different networking events who also want to get more customers. There must be at least one who has a similar target market.

- Connect with an alliance partner and plan a join attraction campaign.

Experience how it feels to use one or several prospect attraction strategies from the Attraction Trifecta to prospect differently. Then watch your contacts respond to you and experience some immediate successes.

Choose Your Prospect Attraction Strategy

Choose one prospect attraction strategy from the Attraction Trifecta that feels most comfortable to you and that you can easily do tomorrow. (And if you want to choose two to get started with because you're an over-achiever like me, good for you!)

Here's a quick list of the attraction strategies again to choose your first one.

Personal Attraction Strategies

1. Email

2. Letters

3. Post cards and other variations of letters and emails

4. Personal networking

5. Phone pursuit

Digital Attraction Strategies

1. E-newsletters

2. Articles and blogs

3. Social networking

4. Social media

Collaborative Attraction Strategies

1. Online PR

2. Online events

3. Local events

4. Offline PR

5. Alliance Partners

Use Your Resources

Remember there are lots of resources for you in the Sales Magnet Tool Kit. I've listed them in the appendix so you can find them quickly. Use them to guide you in your prospect attraction. They'll help you get started, then perfect your Attraction Trifecta.

Take the Next Step

Once you've launched your prospect attraction activities you can step back and perfect your approach. Take the next step and create a campaign that includes several strategies from the

Trifecta. Because people respond to different approaches, this can only increase your response rates.

As more hot prospects begin clicking, emailing, and reaching out to you, you'll be pulled in by the Attraction Trifecta. "The Sales Magnet" approach to prospecting will be too hard to resist. Take the plunge and go get the customers you deserve! Before you know it you will have become a Sales Magnet yourself!

Share Your Successes

I love to hear about my readers' successes. Please share yours with me at www.klagroup.com/sharemysuccess.

I'll post your success story on our blog so other readers can learn from your achievements. (And who knows, you may make some new connections in your target market!)

Acknowledgements

Thank you to our clients and friends for all the ideas and examples that went into this book: sharing what's worked and what hasn't in your prospect attraction; being brave enough to try my suggestions even when they didn't feel comfortable; adjusting your strategies at my recommendation; sharing new techniques you discovered that I hadn't thought of; and celebrating your successes with me! You are a delight to work with!

Thank you to my family for allowing me to encroach upon our special time together to write. You allowed me to push the boundaries when I had a chapter that just had to be written, aching to get out. Without your support and encouragement I couldn't have managed my time to do this.

Thank you to our alliance partners who've expanded their skills to learn new ways to attract prospects, embraced the strategies in their own businesses, and now teach our clients how to do the same. I'm honored to have you as part of our team.

Thank you to my many coaches for pushing me, allowing me to test ideas and keeping me focused on the purpose of this book: to guide other sellers in generating more qualified prospects for their businesses.

Thank you to my editorial and design team for taking my words and ideas and making them visually appealing! Your creativity is simply amazing!

Finally, a special thanks to you, the reader, for the excitement you feel in discovering and testing new methods to attract more prospects who genuinely want and need your expertise. I look forward to hearing of your wins in the Trifecta!

Sales Magnet
Tool Kit Appendix

* * * * * * * * * * * * * * * * * *

This book includes a wealth of resources to help you attract more qualified prospects for yourself. Check out www. thesalesmagnet.com for the tools listed in this book.

As I uncover new ideas and strategies for attracting prospects, I'll post them there, too. So be sure to subscribe and get the latest techniques to use in your prospect attraction strategies.

Chapter 1—Why Prospecting is No Picnic

The Quota Gap Calculator

Chapter 5—Connect Your Efforts

The Campaign Planner

Chapter 6—Make an Offer They Can't Refuse

"Top 10 PowerProspecting Tips"

Chapter 7— Email Prospecting

Email PowerProspecting Sales Kit
Email address list-building resources

Chapter 10—Postcards & Other Variations of Letters

List of unusual holidays you could use for prospect attraction

Chapter 12—Phone Pursuit

PowerProspecting Sales Kit

Chapter 14—Articles and Blogging

A list of websites to post articles for free

Index

Made in the USA
San Bernardino, CA
17 October 2017